BENNETT OATES

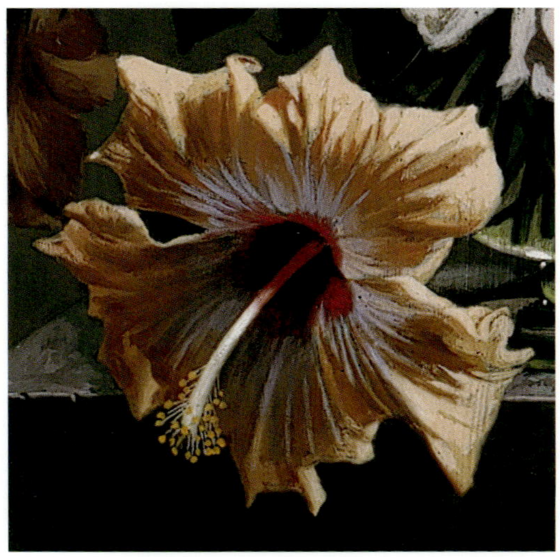

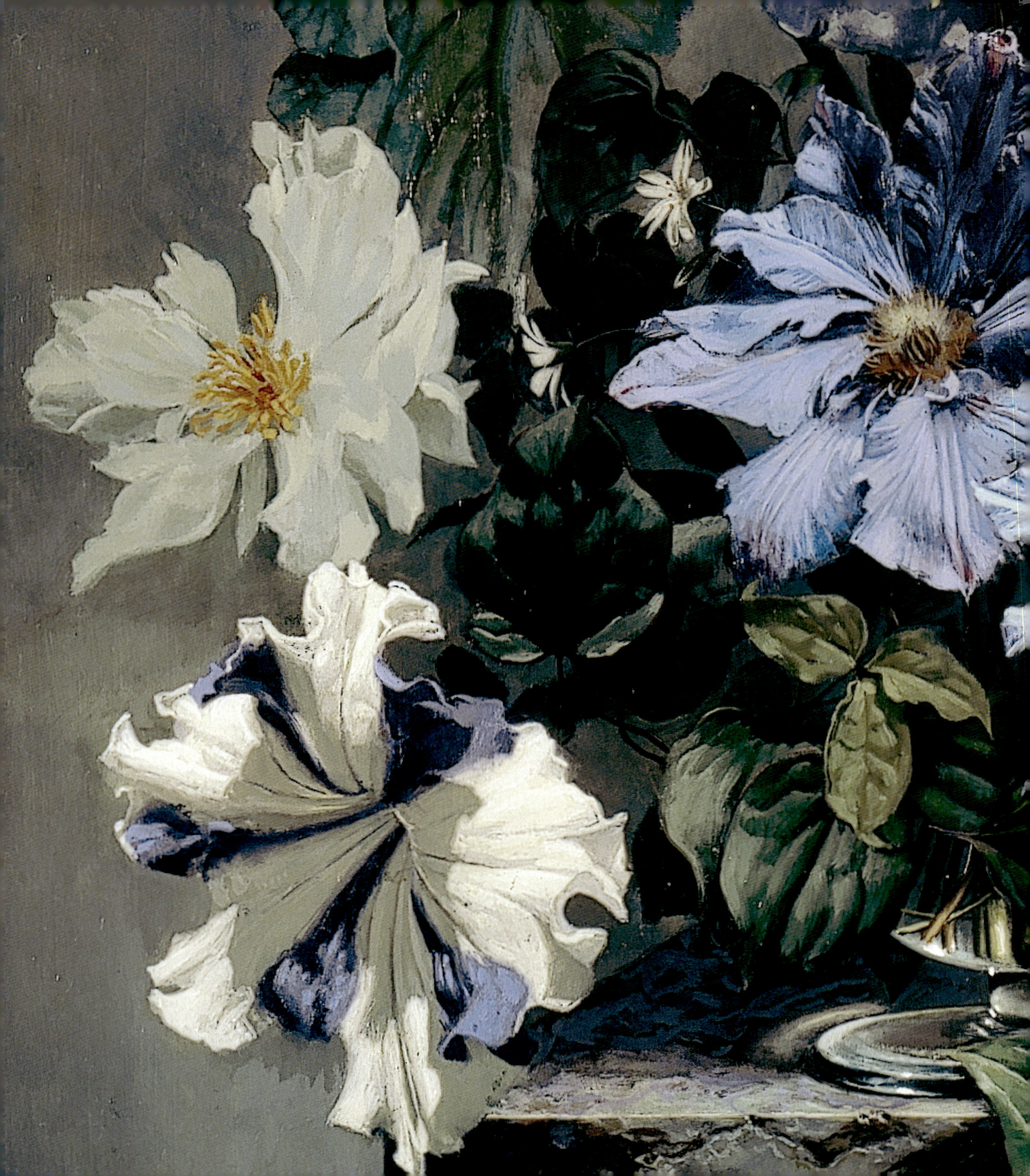

BENNETT OATES

FLOWER PAINTER

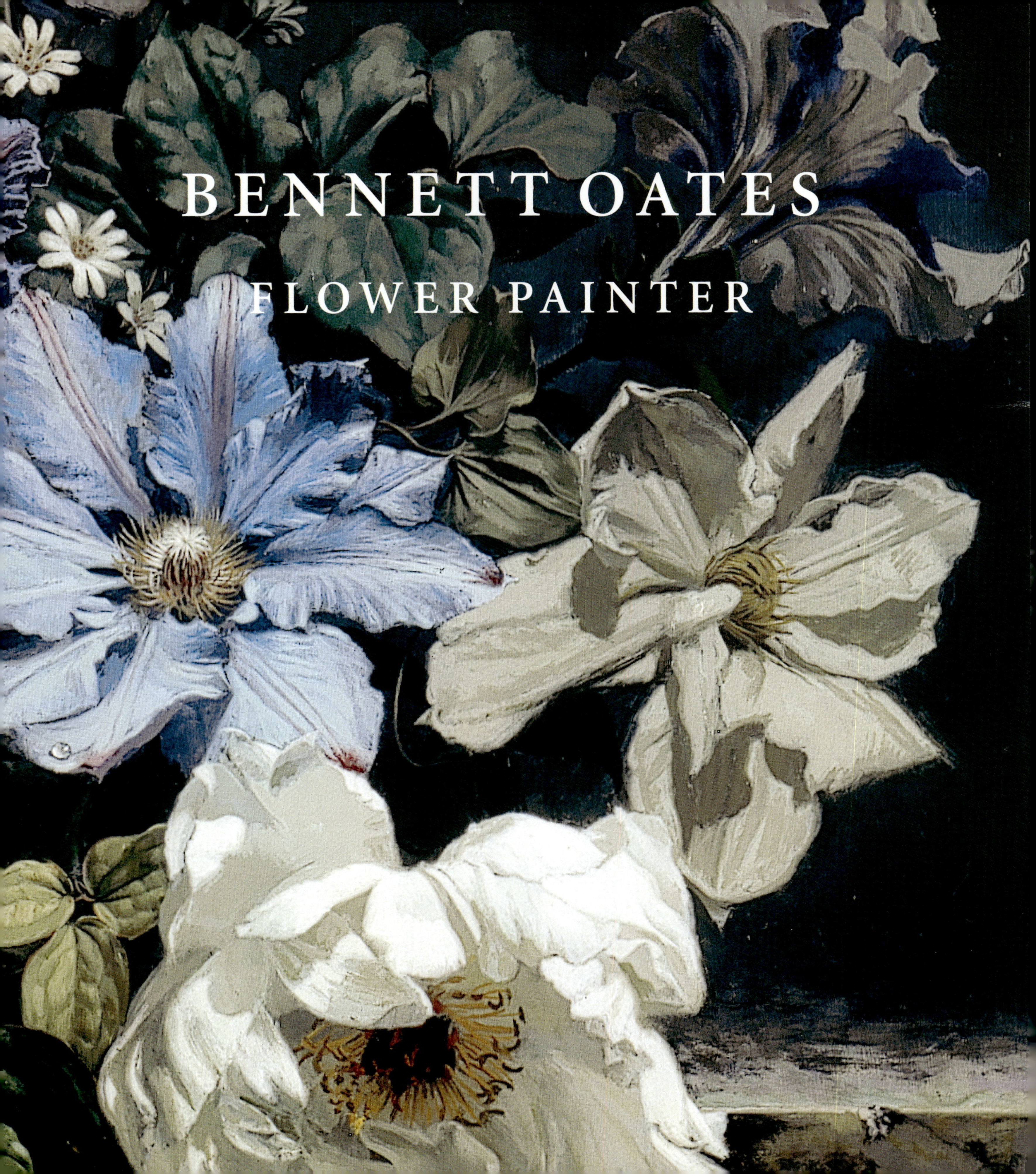

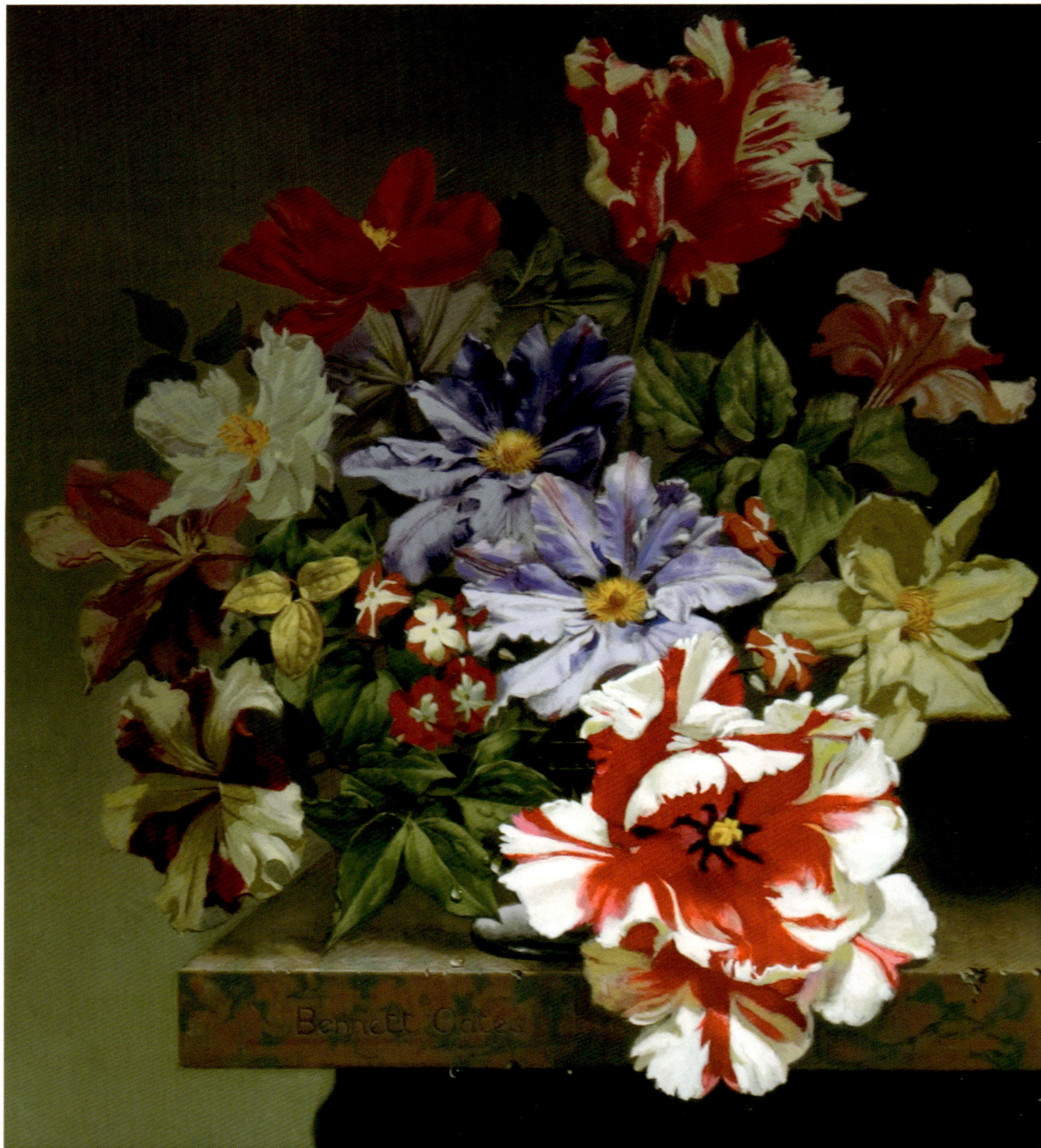

FOREWORD

by Ian Collins

Prized flower paintings by Bennett Oates are usually illuminated by a bright light picking out the best blooms in a brilliant bouquet. It is a ray of revelation. Light emphasises the surrounding shade and, captured at that instant of fullest blossoming, flowers are seen in these studies at their most beautiful, poignant and powerful – at the moment before they fade.

In Persian the word for garden and paradise is the same, but in the former nothing is eternal save for the cycle of birth, growth, decay and regeneration. We love what vanishes but fleeting flowers carry the promise of return. Oates, with a nice line in irony, often mocks this sense of passing time by appearing to incise his signature into the enduring monument of a marble ledge. The art of illusion.

The great Dutch flower artists developed a language of flowers, packing their paintings with symbols and using the brevity of blooms as a call to faith. At a time when a single tulip bulb could cost more than a house, flower paintings were also signs of earthly wealth and prestige. Plus, of course, sensual pleasure.

In our hurried and ever-more artificial world there is something infinitely reassuring about the natural cycle, brought to its most showy display in the cultivated blooms beloved of Oates. He picks clematis, hollyhock, hibiscus, peony, petunia, lily, geranium, rose and tulip – the more brazen and blowsy the better.

Jan van Huysum, greatest of all Dutch flower painters, once wrote to a commissioner that a desired painting could not be produced for a year because an essential yellow rose had just wilted. The meticulous still-life studies of Oates, so slowly nurtured, should also teach us the art of patience.

Steeped in art history, this artist is rooted in a particular setting: the woods and tracks of a small estate in rural Norfolk. He may travel from California to Tuscany to record splendid scenes, but his heart lies in the fickle climate – the play of light and shadow and the flow of the seasons – which is England's greatest glory.

Ian Collins writes for the Eastern Daily Press and is the author of books including
Making Waves: The Artists of Southwold and *A Broad Canvas: Art in East Anglia Since 1880.*

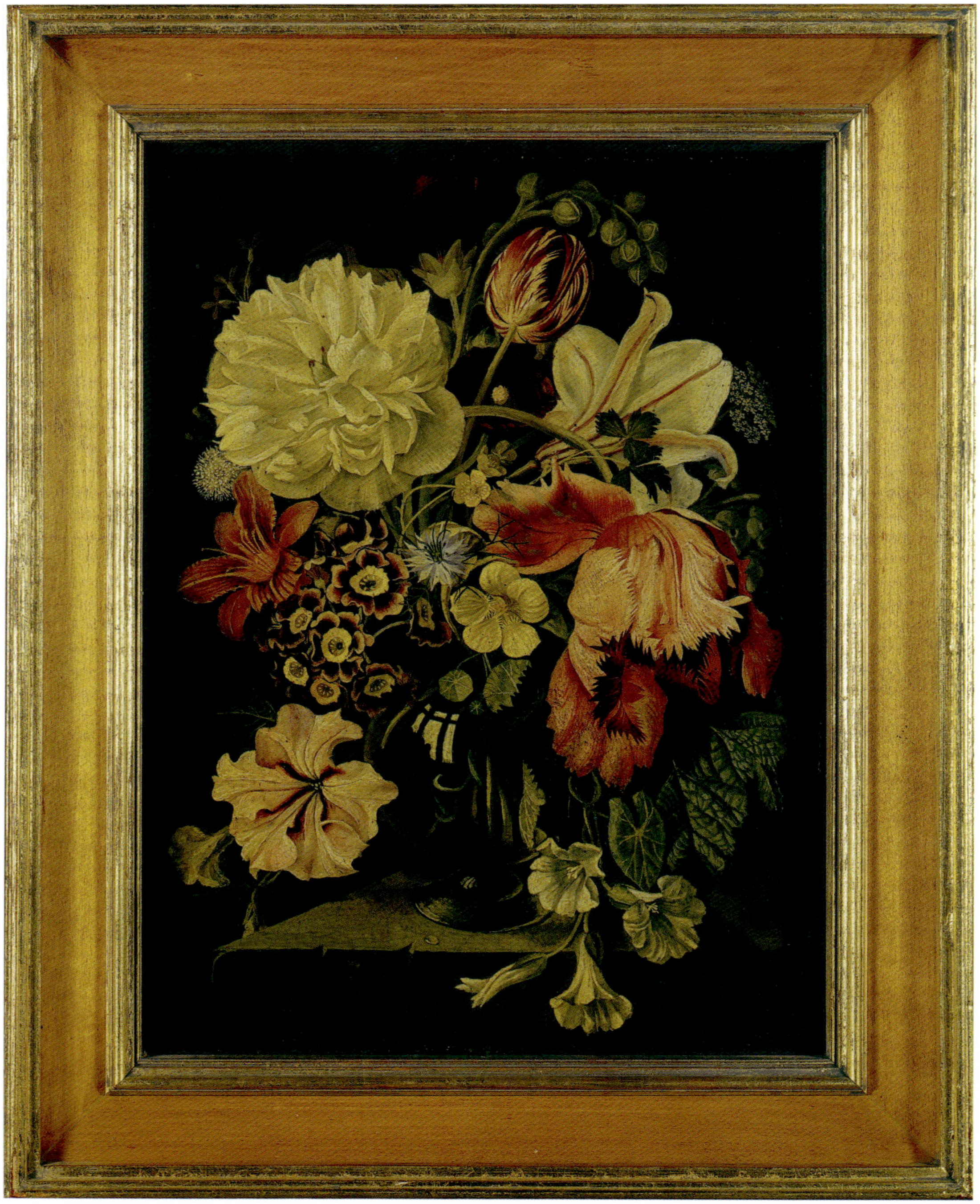

THE BEGINNING

INTRODUCTION

Such is Bennett Oates' talent for painting flower-pieces that each composition creates an aura of perfection. He conjures a true abstract of plants at their peak – in full and delicate maturity. These floral arrangements never existed in reality; many of the blooms are not even in season together.

Yet Oates seals a glorious moment when each flower is in its ideal state. At the same time he builds a fascinating composition that sets off their structure, colour and tone to stunning effect.

To achieve such an illusion with such sureness of touch clearly calls on an innate talent. Oates, in his casually self-mocking style, sums this up with a jibe daubed on the back of one of his early works. Turn over this painting and you find a throwaway line written much later in his career: 'My second flower-piece painted 1944. No subsequent discernable improvement.' (illustrated opposite).

That work, his second still-life of flowers, was sold to his mother for £5 and returned to him when she died. It now hangs among the treasures on the living room wall of his Norfolk home.

The study helps to illustrate another point about Oates and his dedication to being 'a flower painter'. He has been at this game for more than 60 years. It's an achievement to linger on. How has he found the drive to maintain his enthusiasm over three-score years?

The answer lies in that pursuit of perfection that his work so clearly demonstrates. 'An artist must feel a sense of inadequacy in order to keep striving,' he says. So with perfection as the goal, how does Oates know when a painting can be regarded as finished?

First of all, it is important to realise that working in oils allows Oates the luxury of being able to overpaint when he feels things are not going right. If a conservator made X-ray studies of the paintings they would find many layers of 'corrections'.

He also chooses to paint on board. This not only means that the work should be much less susceptible to future degradation than if it were applied to canvas, but it allows Oates to be so much more precise in applying the paint. Whereas a brushstroke will soften and lose some of its definition as it is delivered on to a giving canvas, more clarity can be achieved when working on unyielding board.

The work is complete 'when it satisfies my eye, or the moment before I put my foot through it', Oates confides. To reach this point, when things go well, can take as little as ten days.

On the other hand, it can take up to three months. 'You have to keep going back. You can't understand why it doesn't work, then suddenly it comes to you and you realise how to make it work.'

Oates ensures that he can remain focused and enthusiastic in his studio by escaping to the great outdoors and allowing his eye and his brushes free rein. The results are what he terms his 'poetic studies'. In contrast to the detailed control of the flower-pieces, here free brushwork reveals a more romantic side to Oates' talents.

All nature's moods are explored; from an exuberant rush of yellow on wild gorse in sunlit heathland, to the shadowy intimacy of a woodland walk. The seasons, too, offer Oates the opportunity to challenge the palette – from the brilliance of a snow-covered bramble to the subtle dusk of an autumn sunset and the shifting wisps of a late bonfire.

The work is delightfully fresh or as Oates puts it: 'The poetic studies are my chance to get out and splosh some paint around'.

Much of the inspiration for these works stems from Oates' walks with his Bernese mountain dog and Dalmatians in and around the 12 acres of grounds at his home, a former hunting lodge that was once a part of the old Boleyn estate. Here, he and the dogs are able to sniff out the subtle switches in mood of woodland, pasture and a lake. There are unmistakable echoes here of Claude Monet's preoccupation with his familiar surroundings at Argenteuil and the garden at Giverny.

But he has also taken his paints on family holidays abroad, where he has found fresh inspiration in less-familiar territory of France and Italy. Equally, travel has allowed Oates greater opportunities to see original works by, among others, the French impressionist masters Alfred Sisley and Camille Pisarro that have refuelled his enthusiasm for landscapes.

It is a tribute to Oates' talent that he is able to bridge the gap between two such contrasting artistic worlds: to carry on the tradition that first flourished in the stylised flower-pieces created in the studios of 16th- and 17th-century Dutch masters such as Jacob van Huysum, Abraham Mignon and Nicolas van Verendael while revelling in the freedom of a new realm established by the Impressionists of the late 19th century. For Oates the essential link between these two styles is the commitment to 'honest' painting.

There is a rebel in Oates, but so far as his art is concerned it expresses itself in refusing to accept what he regards as the shortcuts and shallowness of modern art. 'My flower-pieces are a reaction against all the gimmickry that is being peddled today,' he says.

This is not the late raging of an ageing artist but a theme that has run throughout his career.

As a student at the Wimbledon College of Art in the 1940s, experimenting with figure work and still-life, Oates was naturally drawn to the work of its principal, the late Gerald Cooper. 'He was the finest living flower painter. He encouraged me to work in the genre,' says Oates.

The Dutch masters had considered flower-pieces the ultimate test of a studio artist's talents. Oates was fascinated with the compositions and the deep understanding of colour they demanded.

While still a teenager he first enjoyed the satisfaction of having one of his paintings hung at the Royal Academy. 'I remember I went back five times that summer to look at it,' he recalls.

His work continued to earn a place in the exhibition over successive years until, as he puts it, 'fashions changed and they didn't want to know about flower painting'. But fashions have not changed among the public, where the quality of his classic pieces has ensured continuing demand.

It was his steadfast belief in the essentials of artistic endeavour that drove Oates to join with three other artists to form the Guild of Norwich Painters in 1992.

The guild, of which Oates is president, is dedicated to perpetuating the best traditions of the old masters. Its membership, now expanded to twelve artists, meets regularly and reflects a heritage, that of the artistic school, which has played such a vital part in enhancing key painting movements.

'The philosophy of the guild is to maintain the standards of draughtsmanship and artistic propriety that to my mind are getting lost or eroded through modern short-cuts and sophistry,' explains Oates.

For all his efforts to foster a greater awareness of the fundamental building blocks of painting, Oates feels that, in his late 70s, he has become something of a 'dinosaur' in the field of flower-pieces as artists have 'turned their backs' on the genre. But he has one particularly reassuring hope for the future – his younger daughter Michelle. Oates, again in a reaction to modern schooling in art, decided that he himself must nurture her obvious talent and so set about teaching her the basics of good drawing and other essentials of painting.

Allowing her to explore her talent through creating still-life studies at home, she developed a love of wildlife painting and became a member of the Society of Wildlife Artists. Latterly, however, married and living in Devon, she has taken on her father's mantle as 'a proficient flower painter' and an example of her work is shown at the end of this book.

Oates and his wife, Phyllis, also have an older daughter, Helen, who studied art history and met her husband, a chief inspector with English Heritage, when she was a librarian there. They now live on the River Fal, in Cornwall, where their teenage son delights in another of Oates' great passions, sailing.

Phyllis met Oates when he went on from his studies at Wimbledon to join the Royal College of Art, where she was studying design and illustration. It was, by the way, her time at the RCA that resulted in her writing *The Story of Western Furniture* – still a set text in courses around the world today.

A natural 'eye' for art and a deep understanding of her husband's work have led to her adopting a twin role, both as the strongest supporter of his endeavours and his best critic. No painting leaves the studio without reference to her views.

When contemplating producing this book, Oates joked: 'It should be entitled "Dinosaur"'. But, more than anything else, this book illustrates a talent that delivers artistic truth. Here are paintings of such quality that, unlike those dusty dinosaur bones, they will stand the test of time and sing out a resonating celebration of life for future generations.

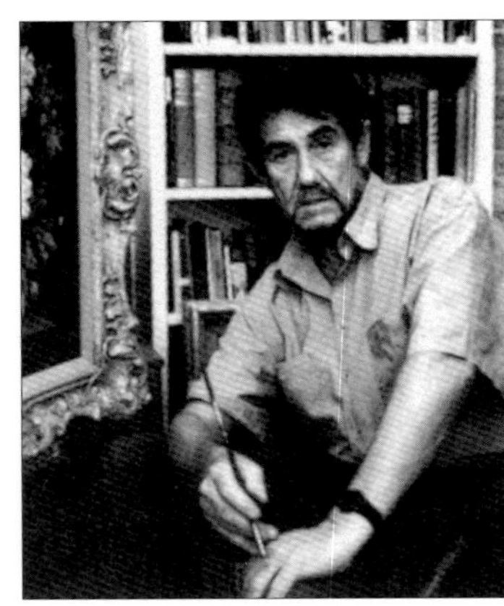

FLOWERS

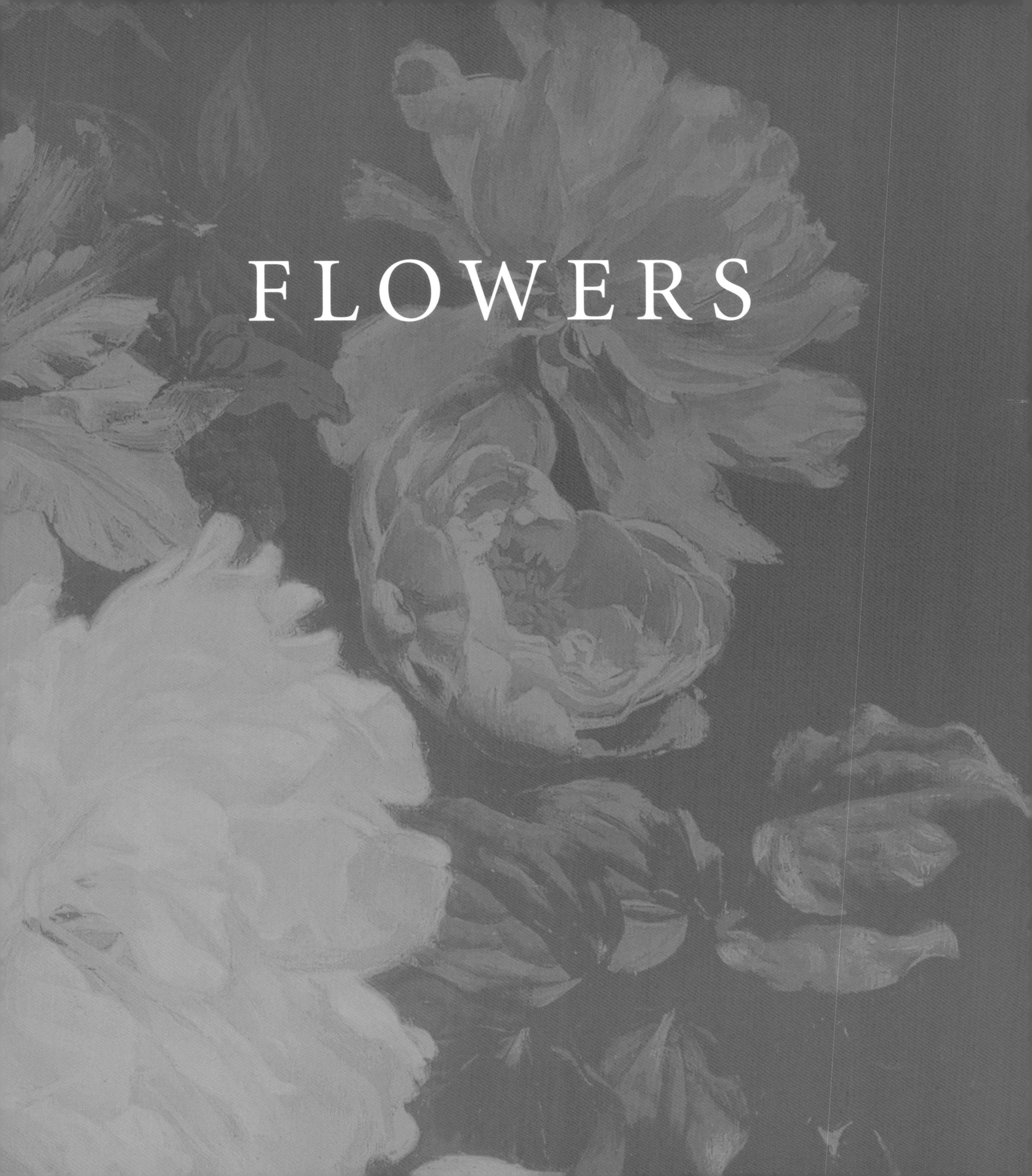

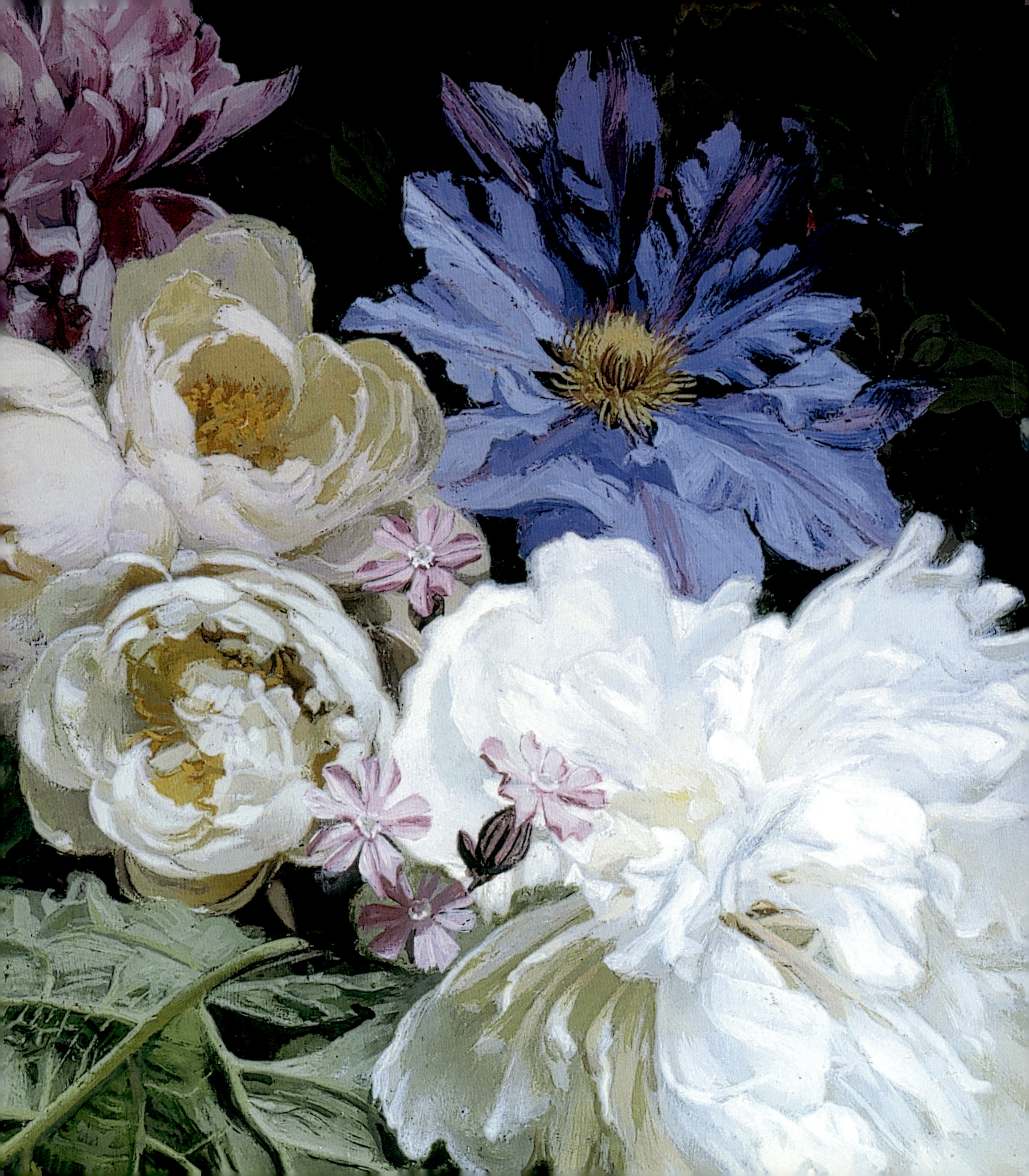

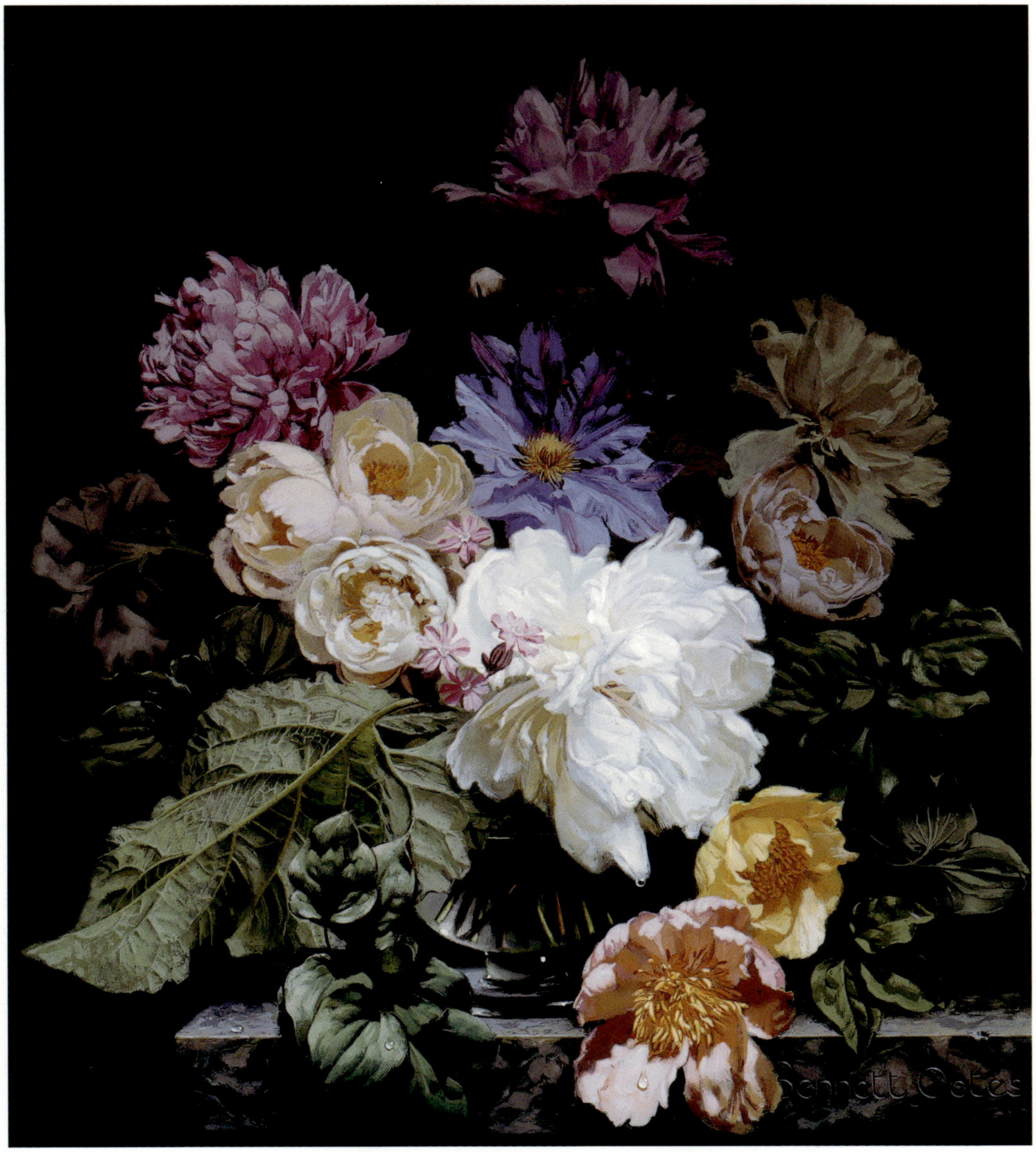

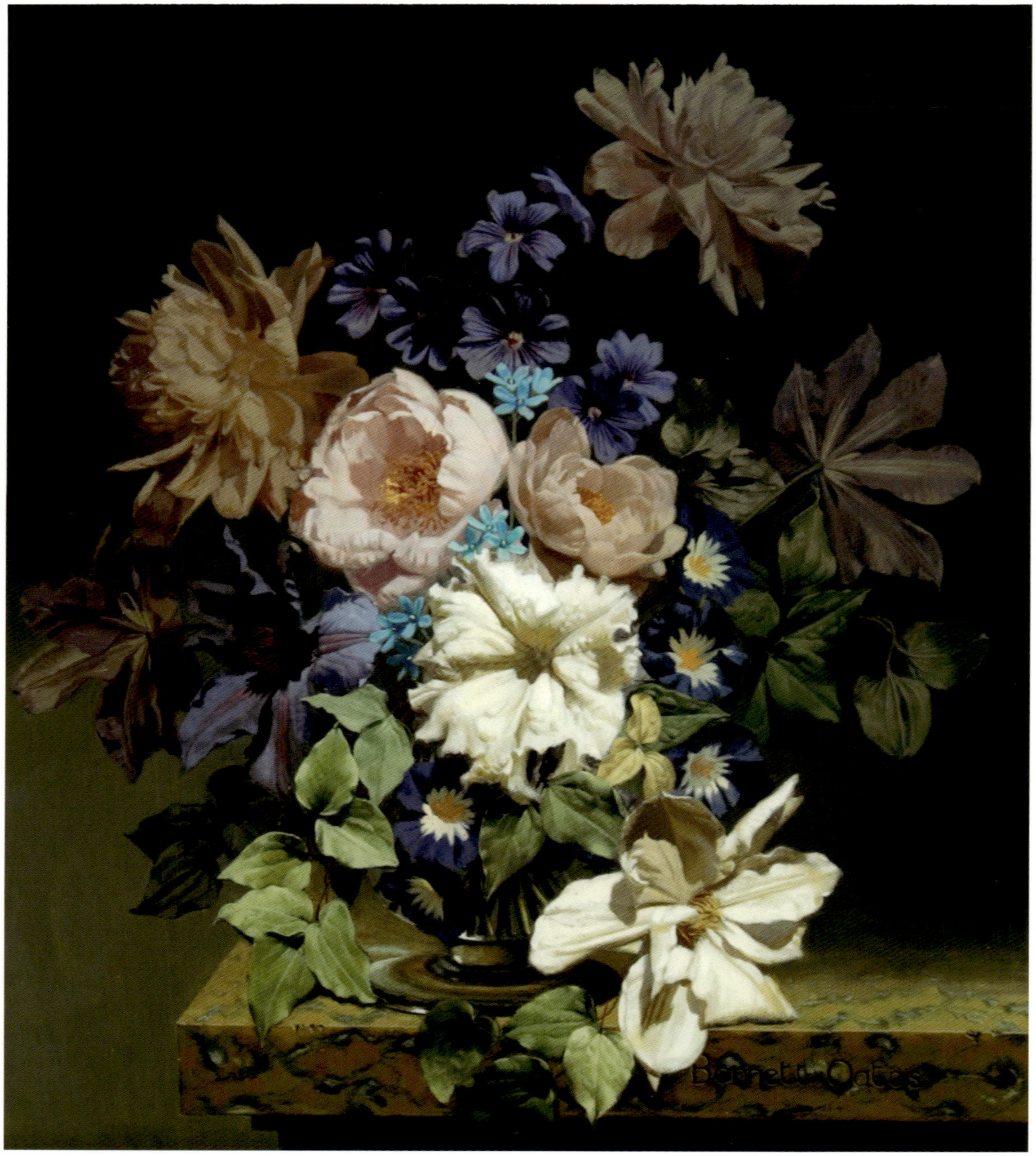

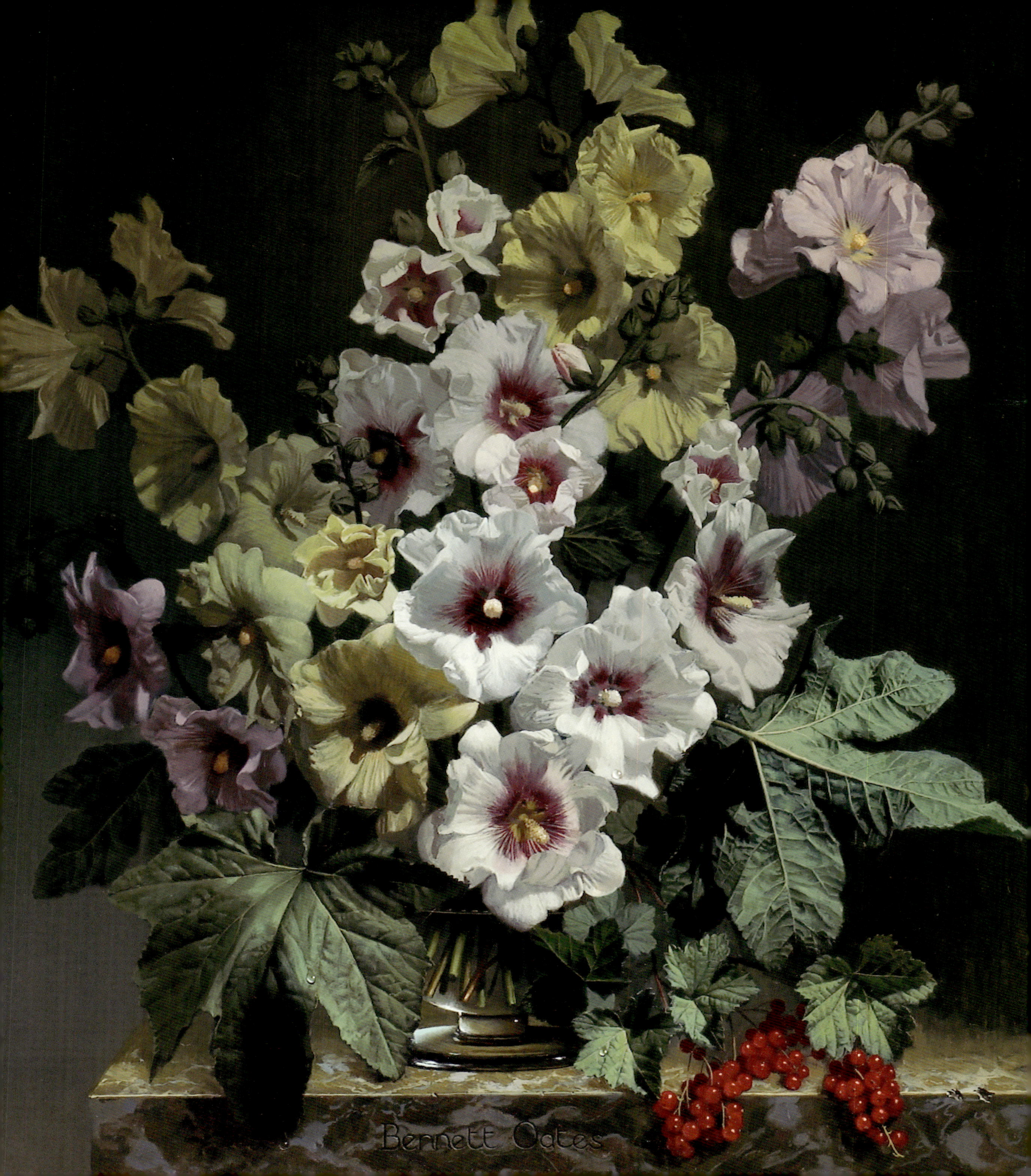
Bennett Oates

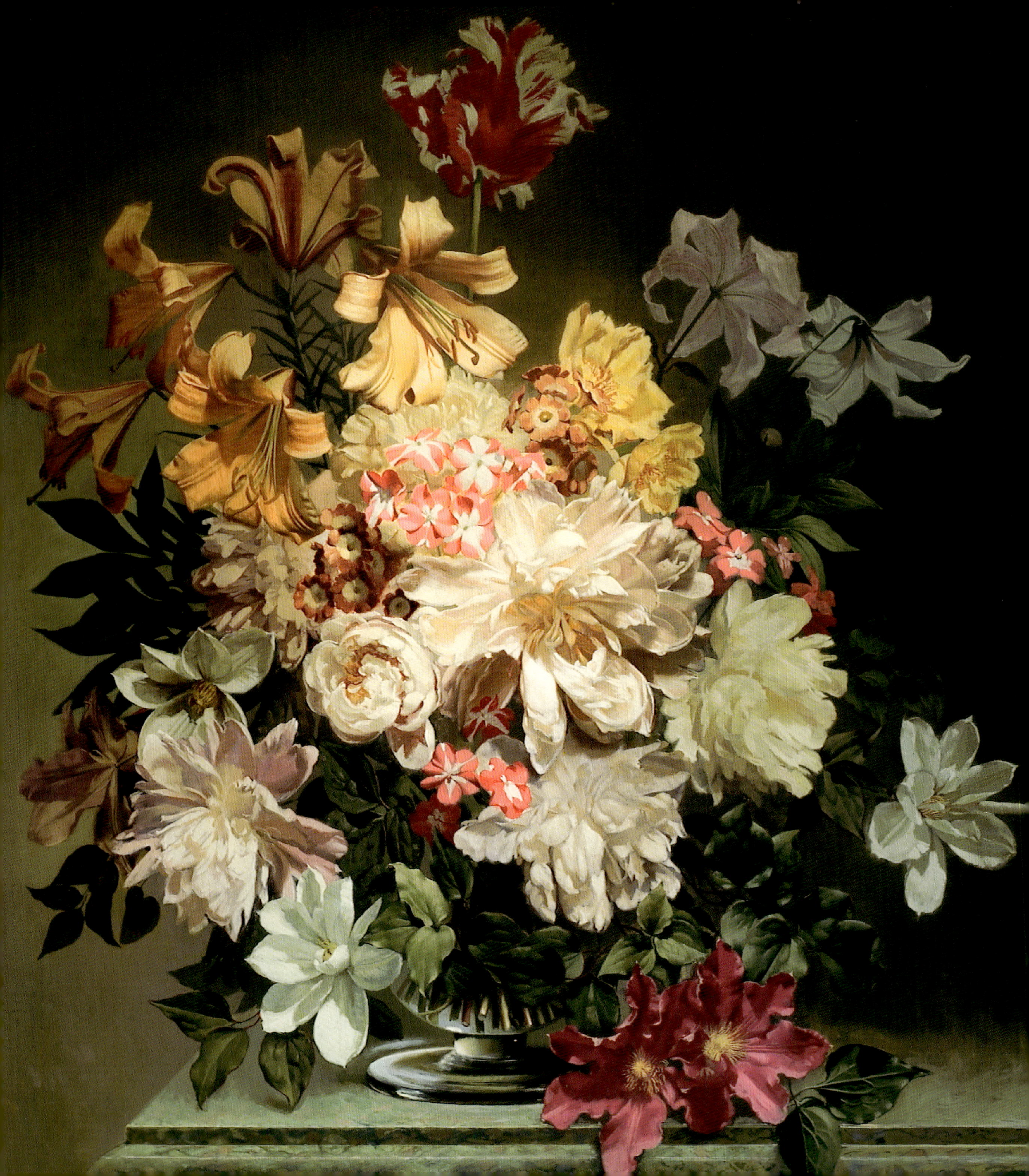

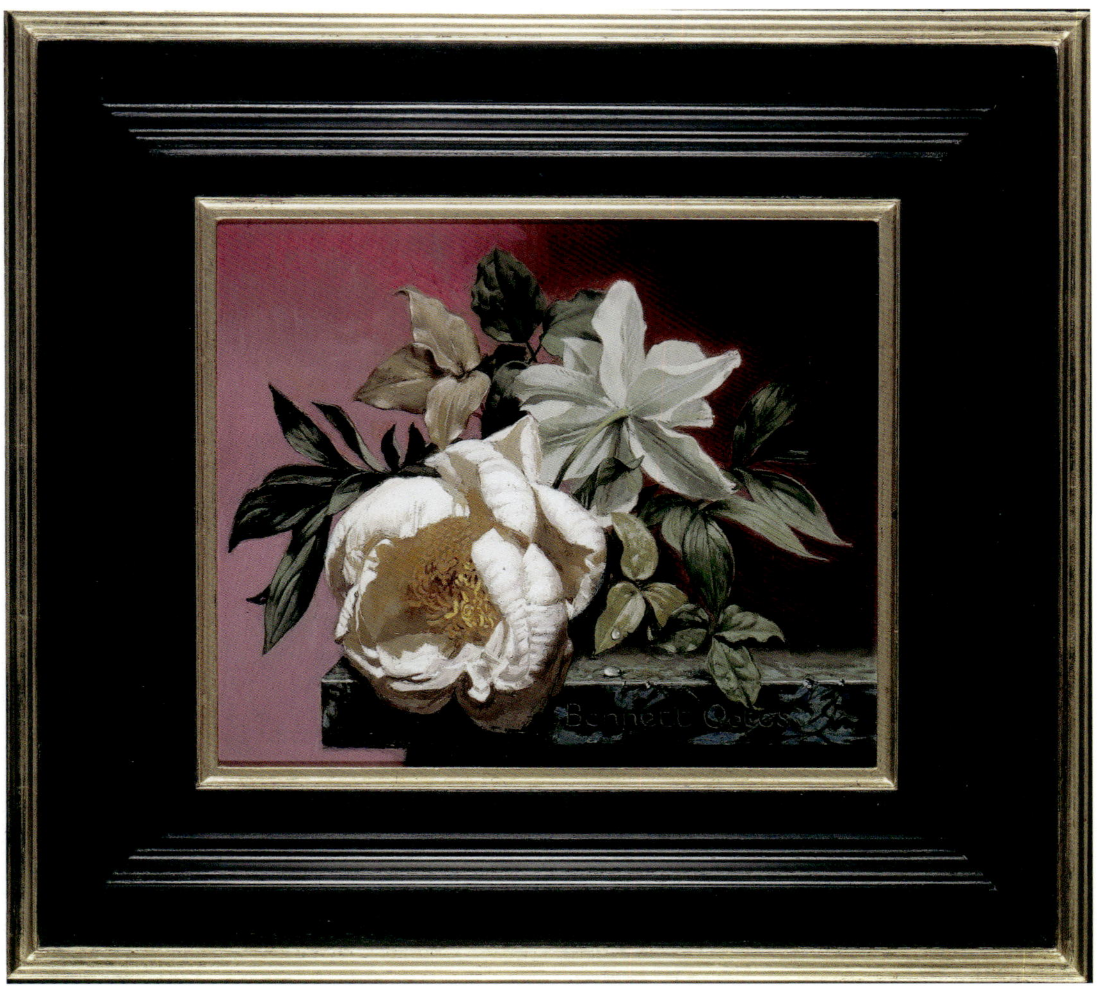
Bennett Oates

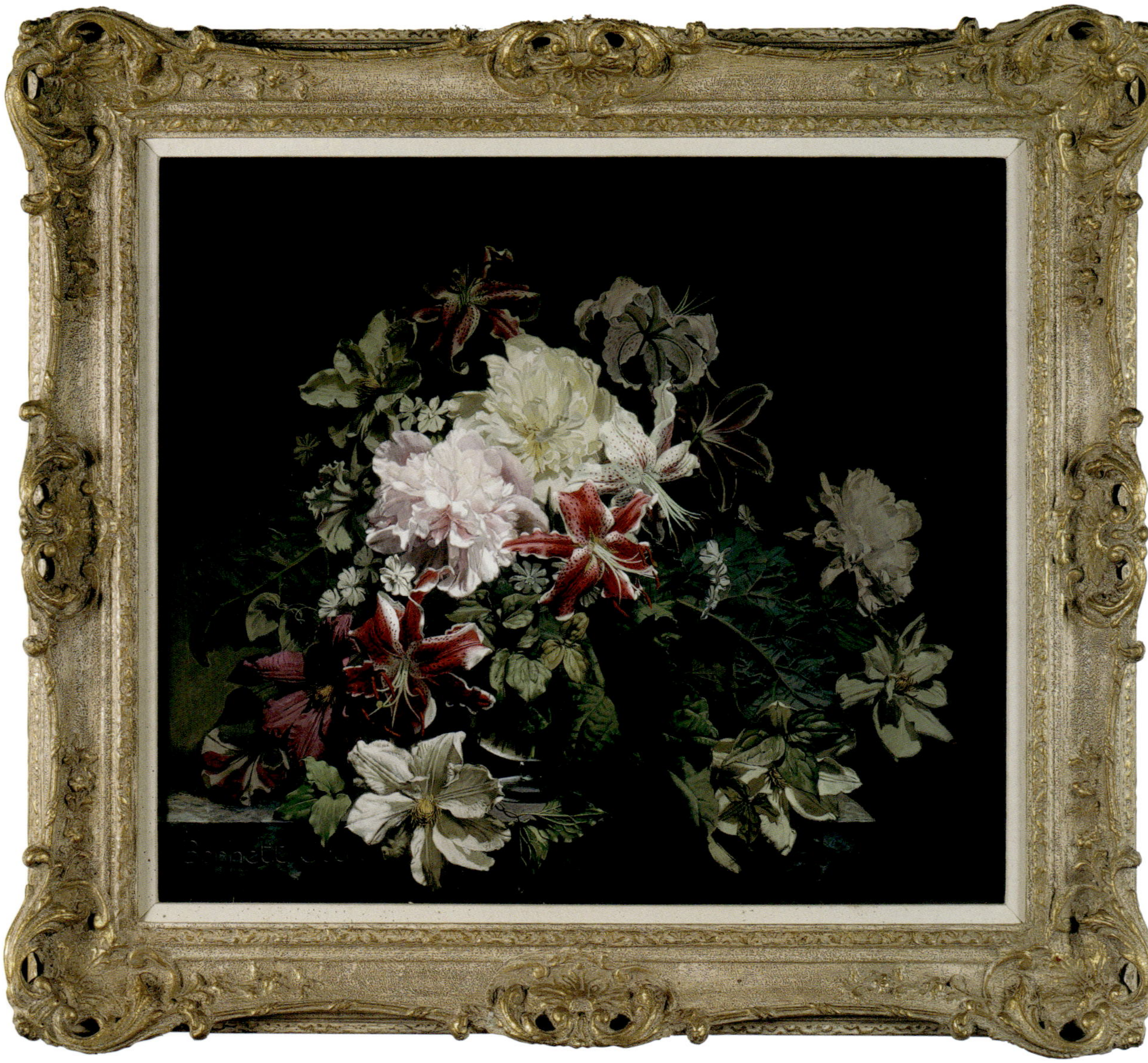

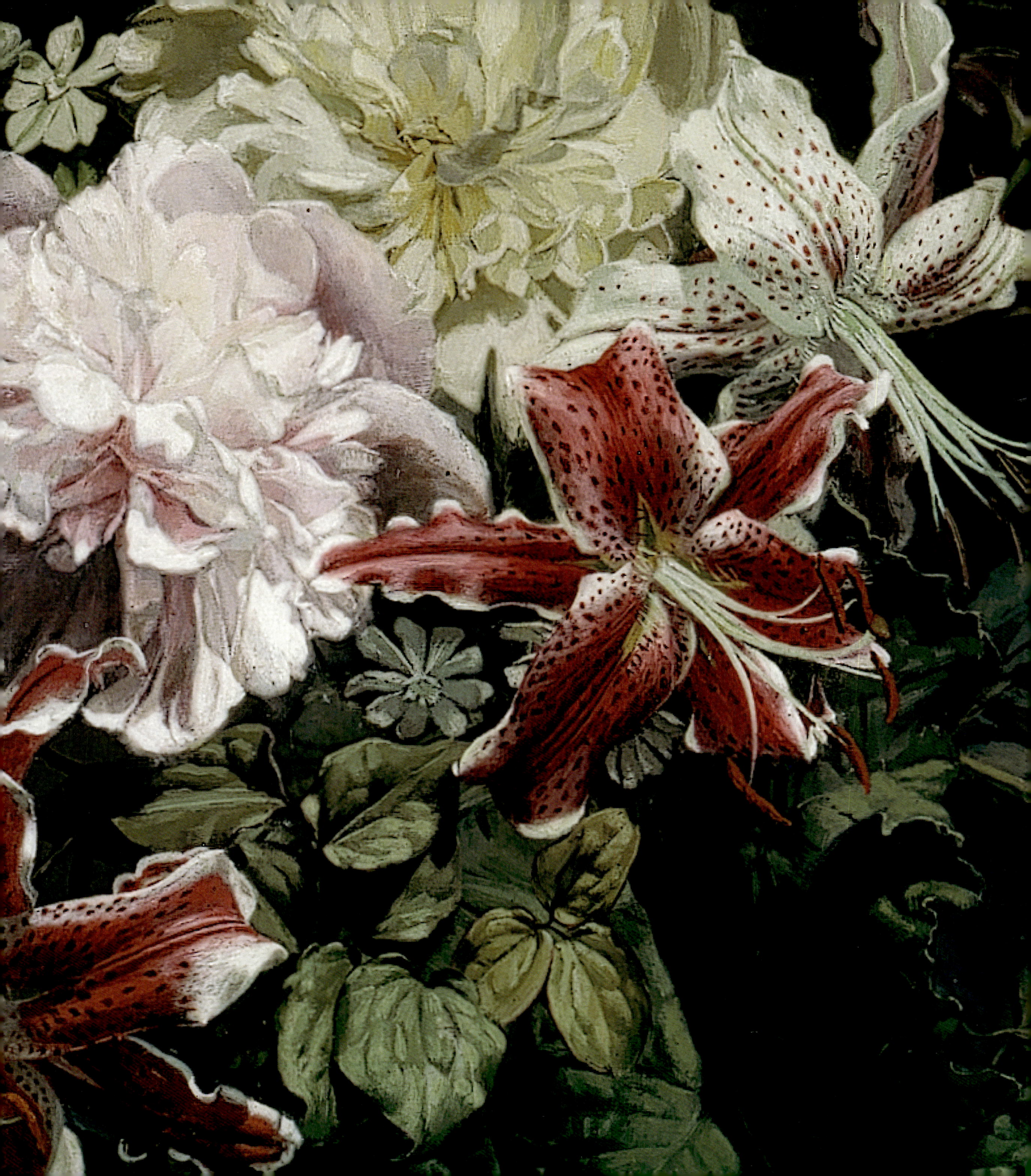

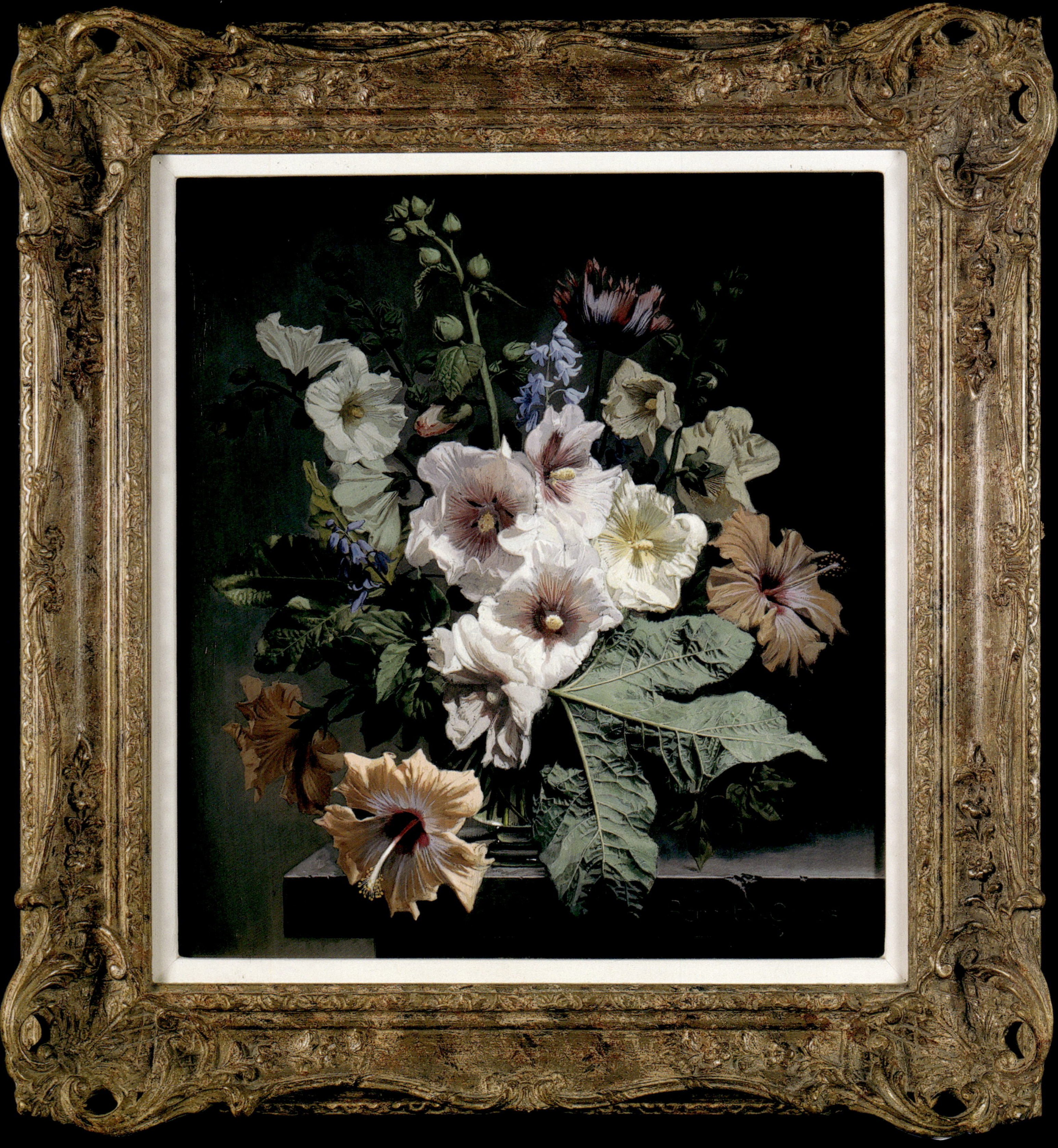

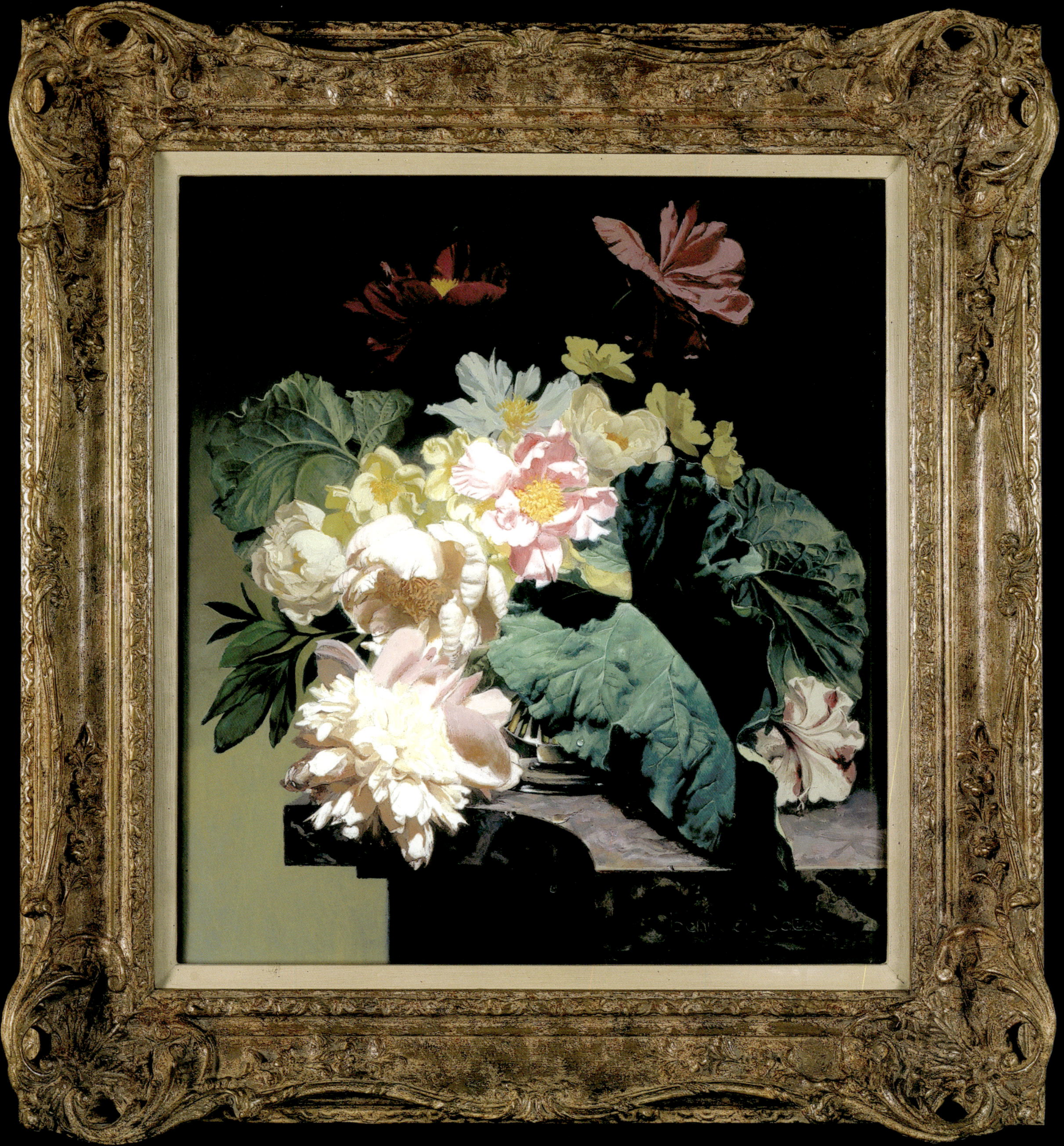

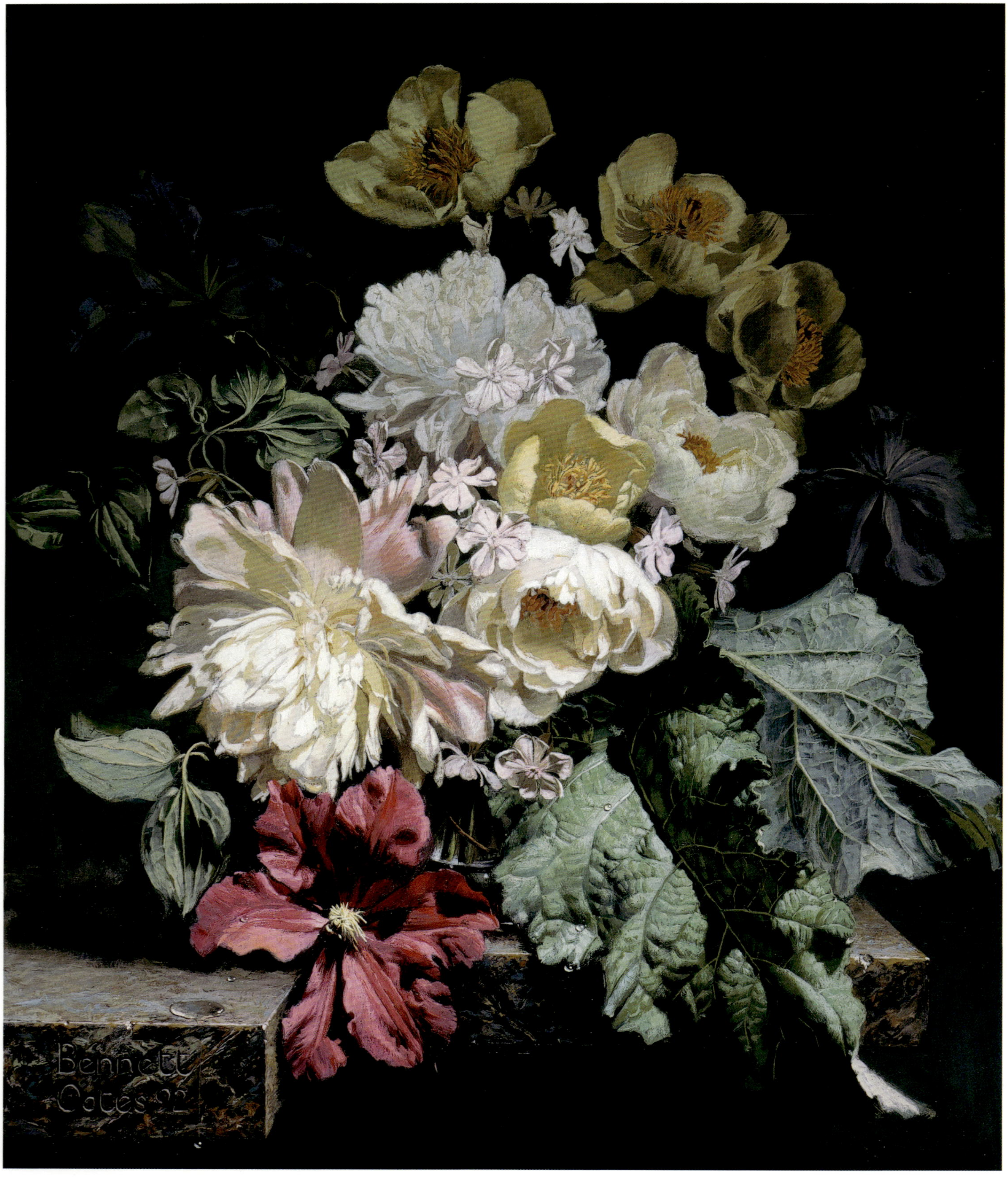
Bennett
Oates 92

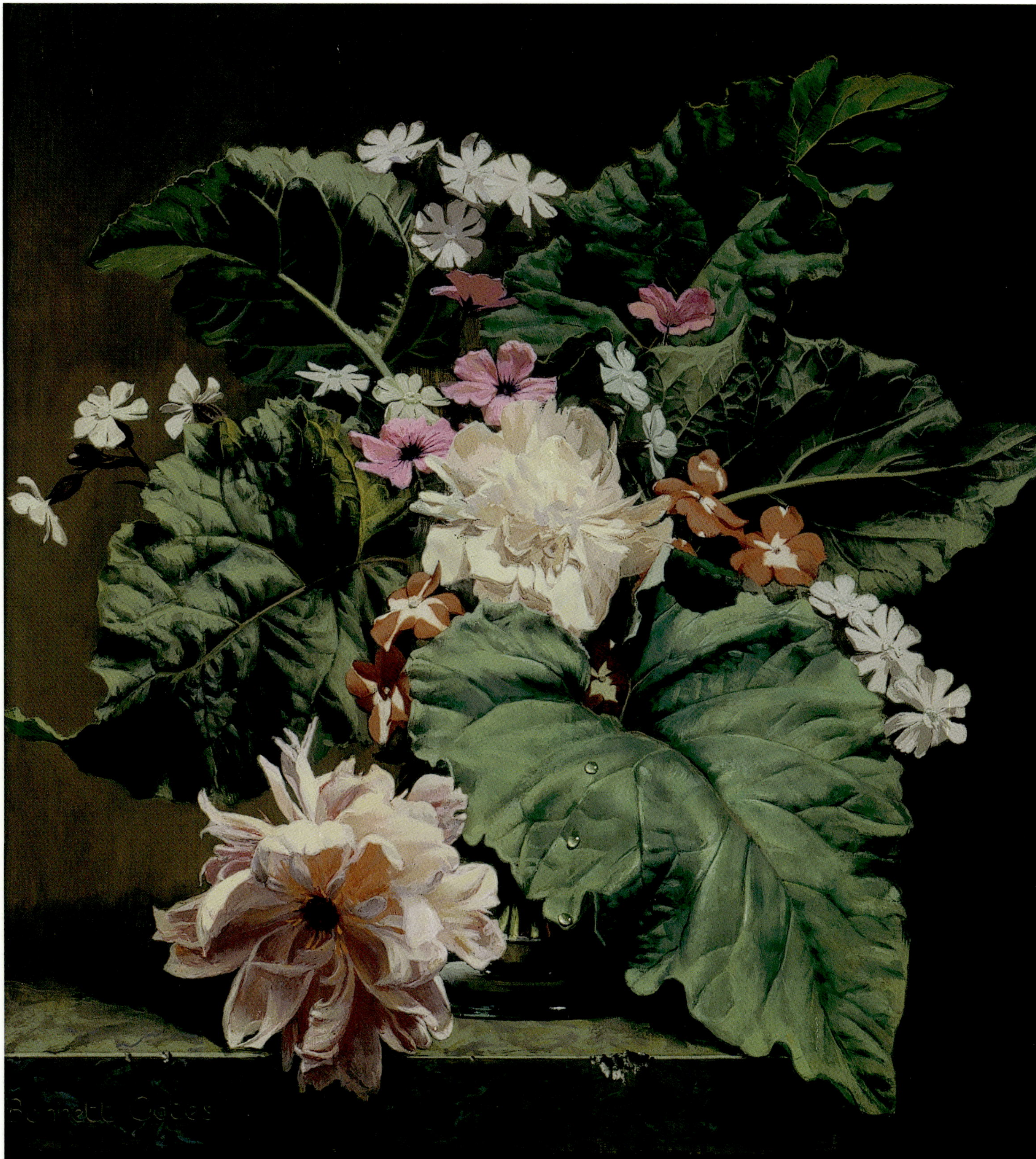

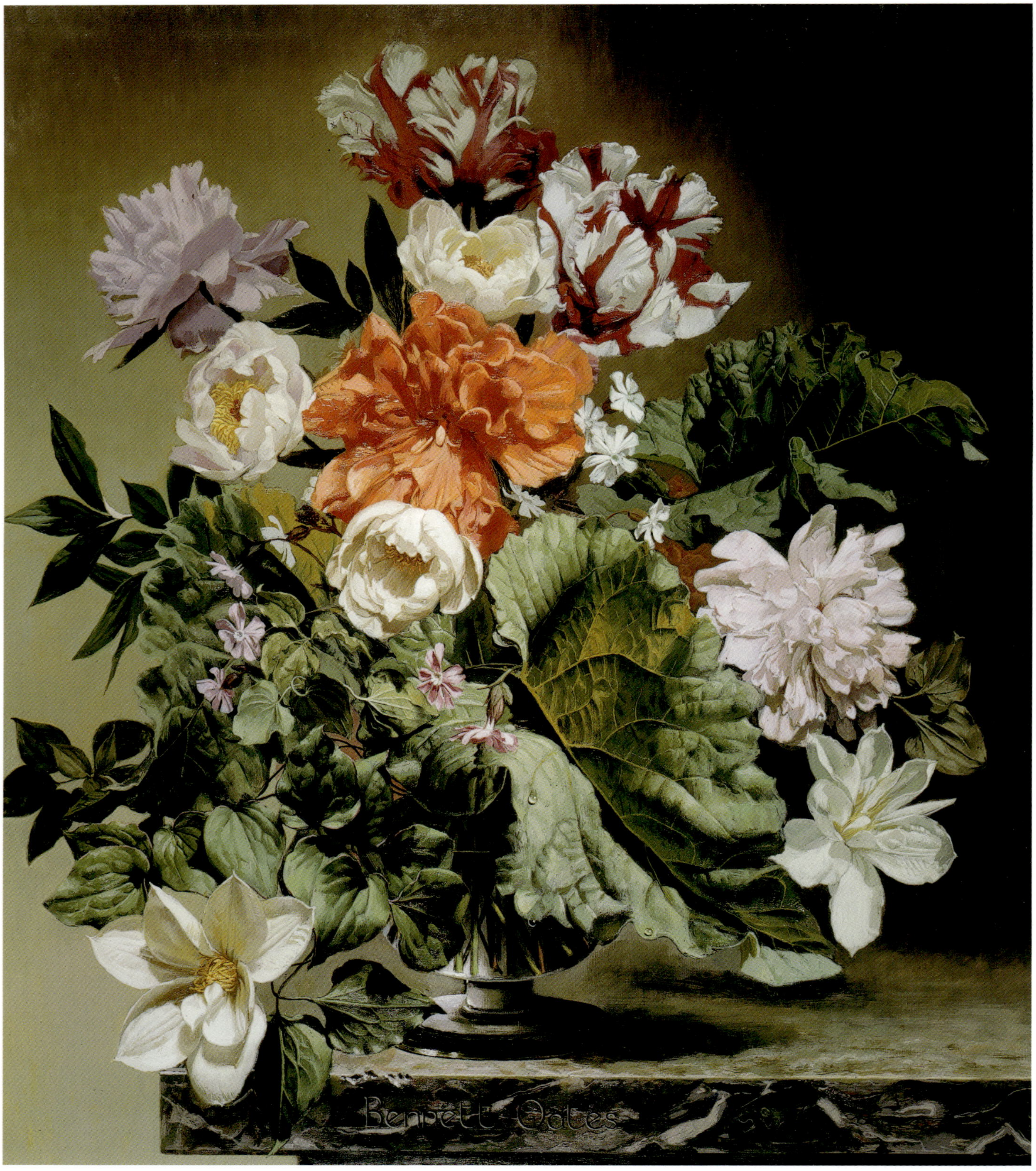
Bennett Oakes

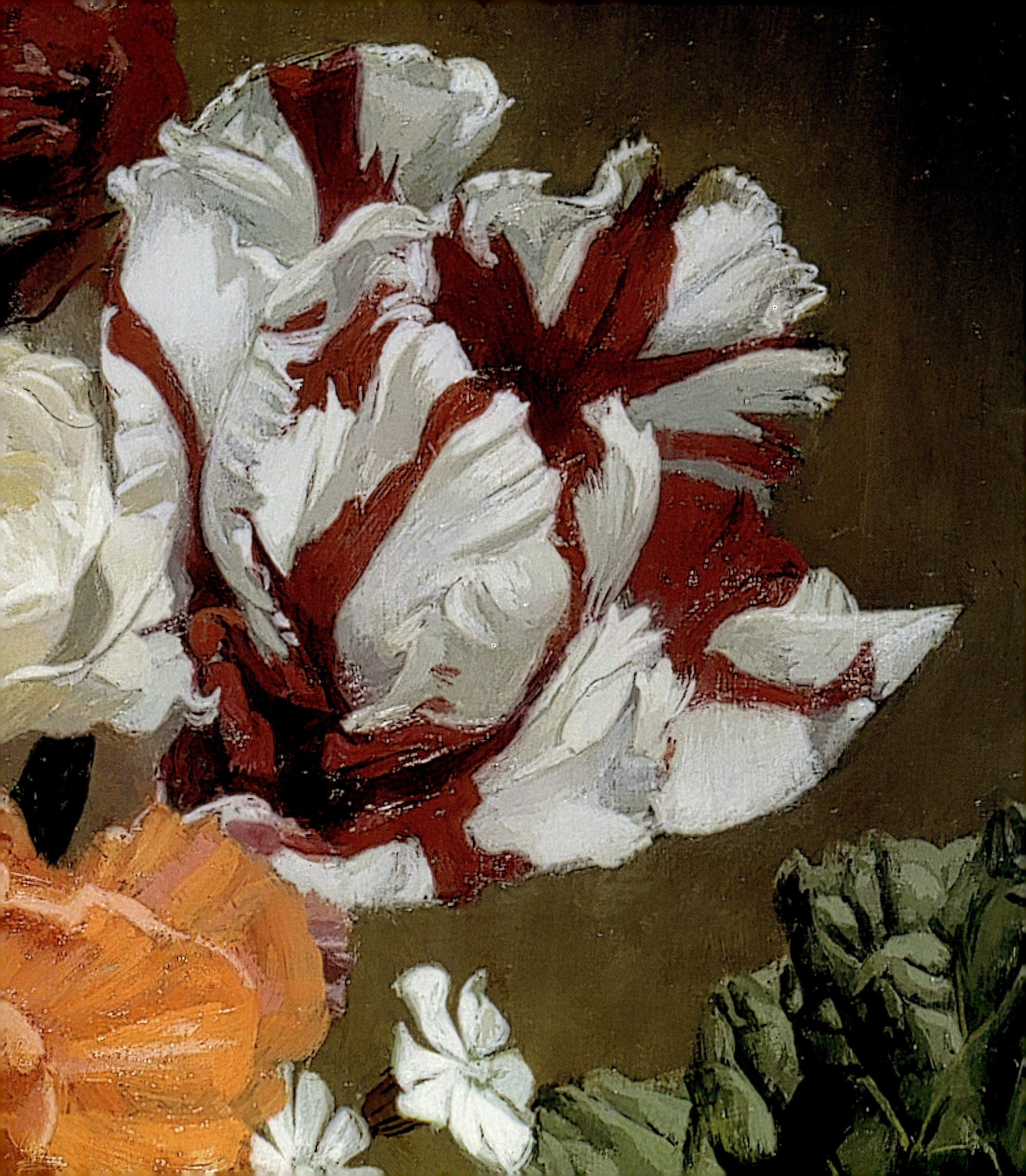

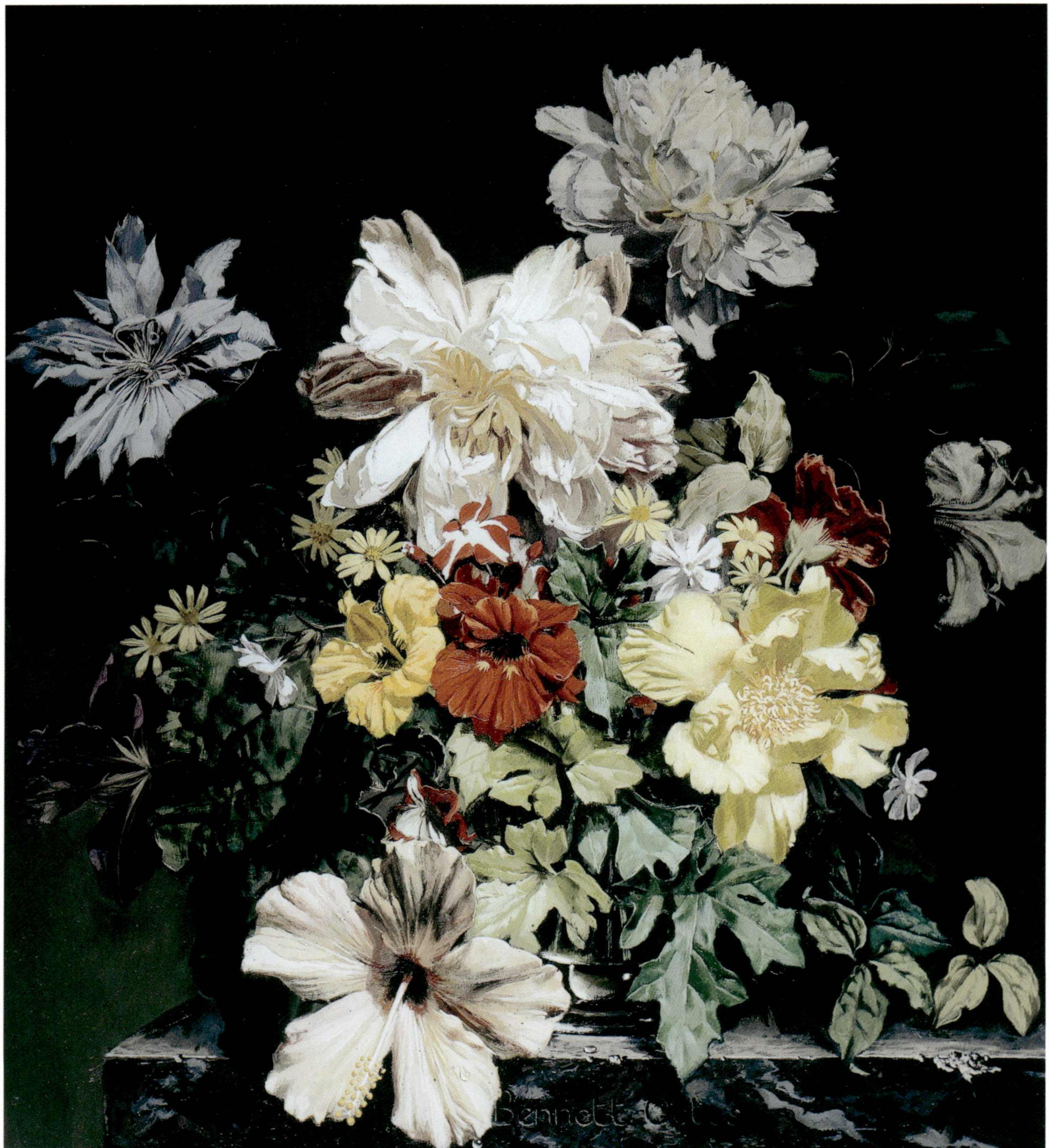
Bennett

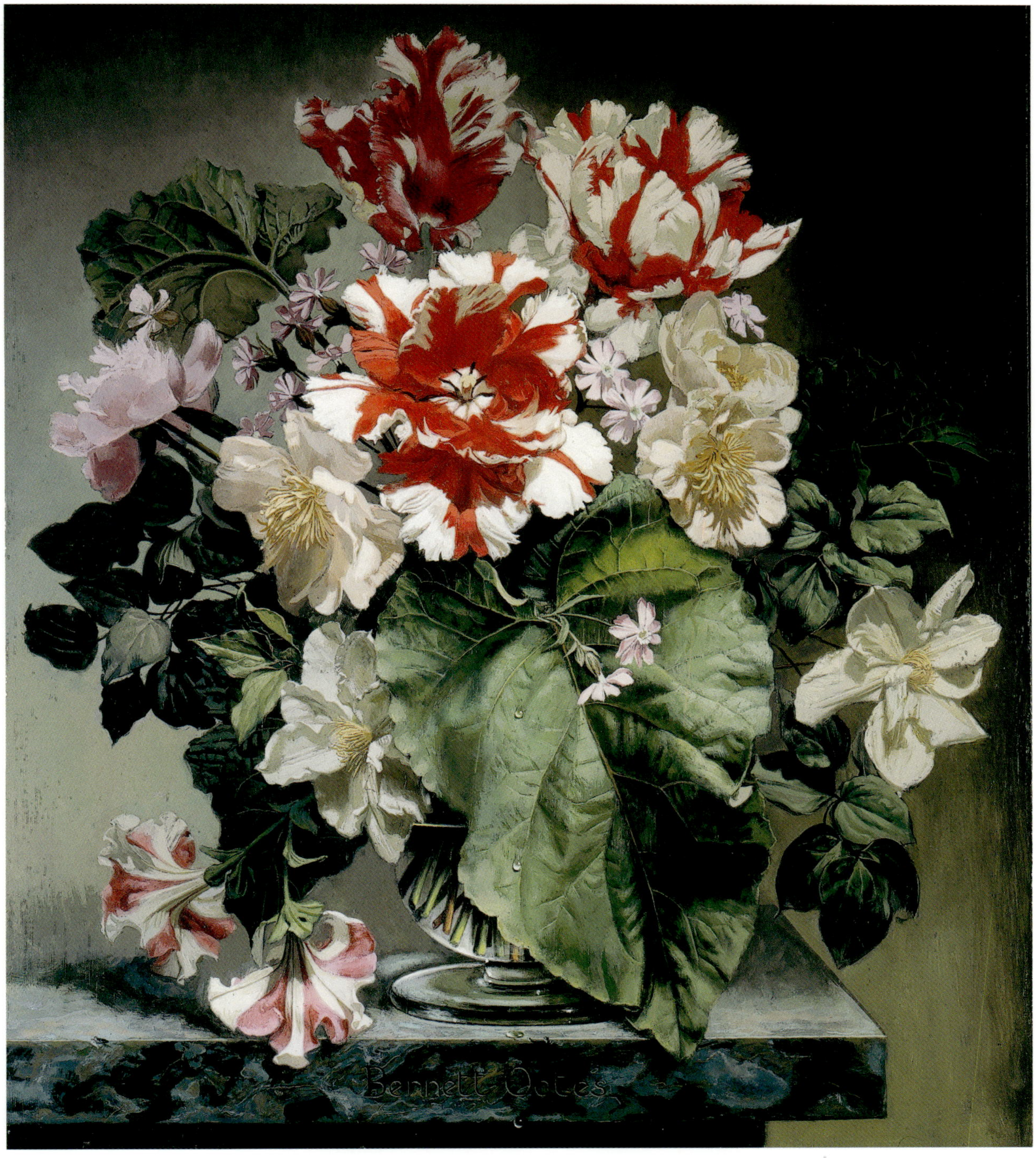
Bennett Oates

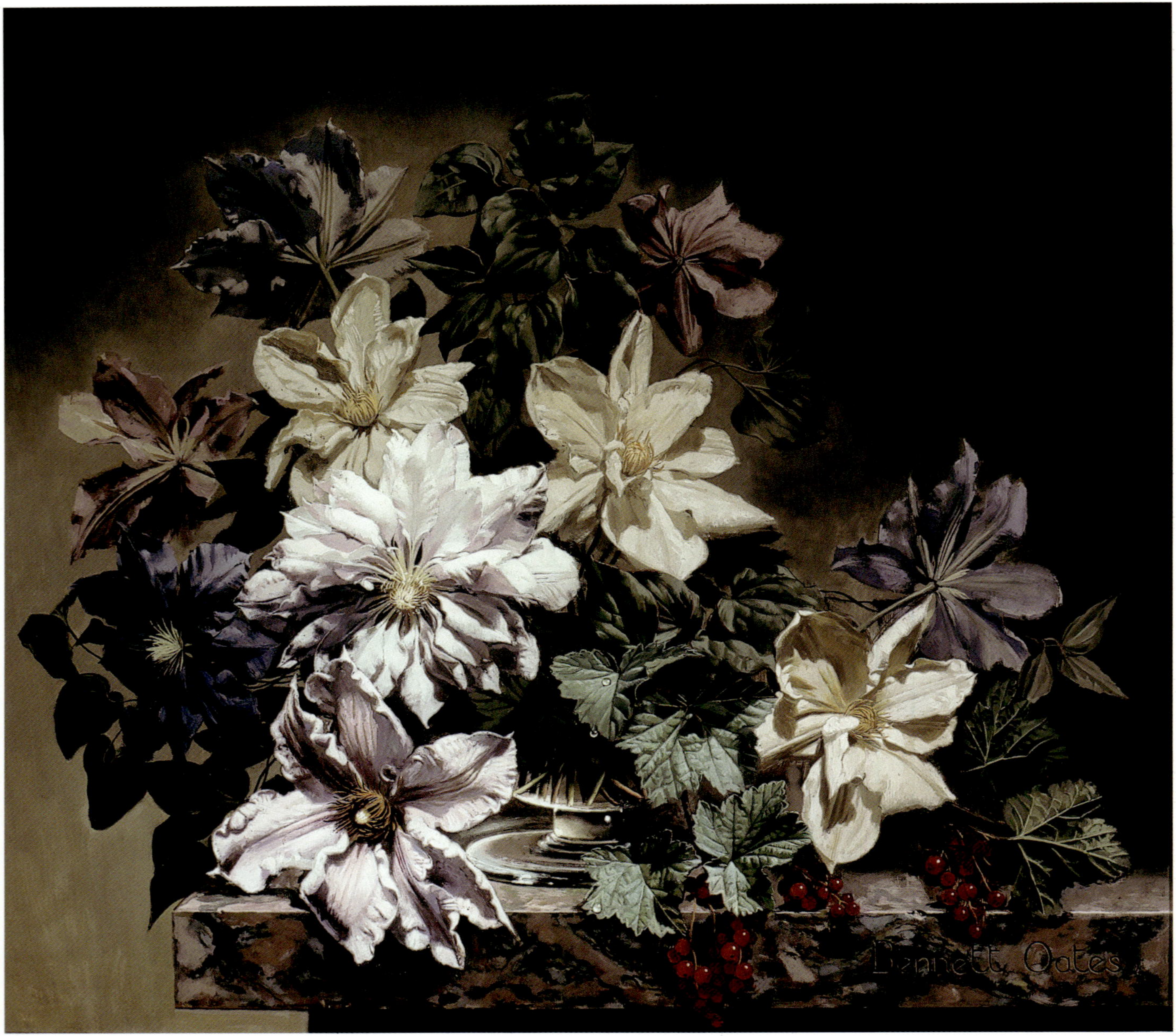
Bennett Oates

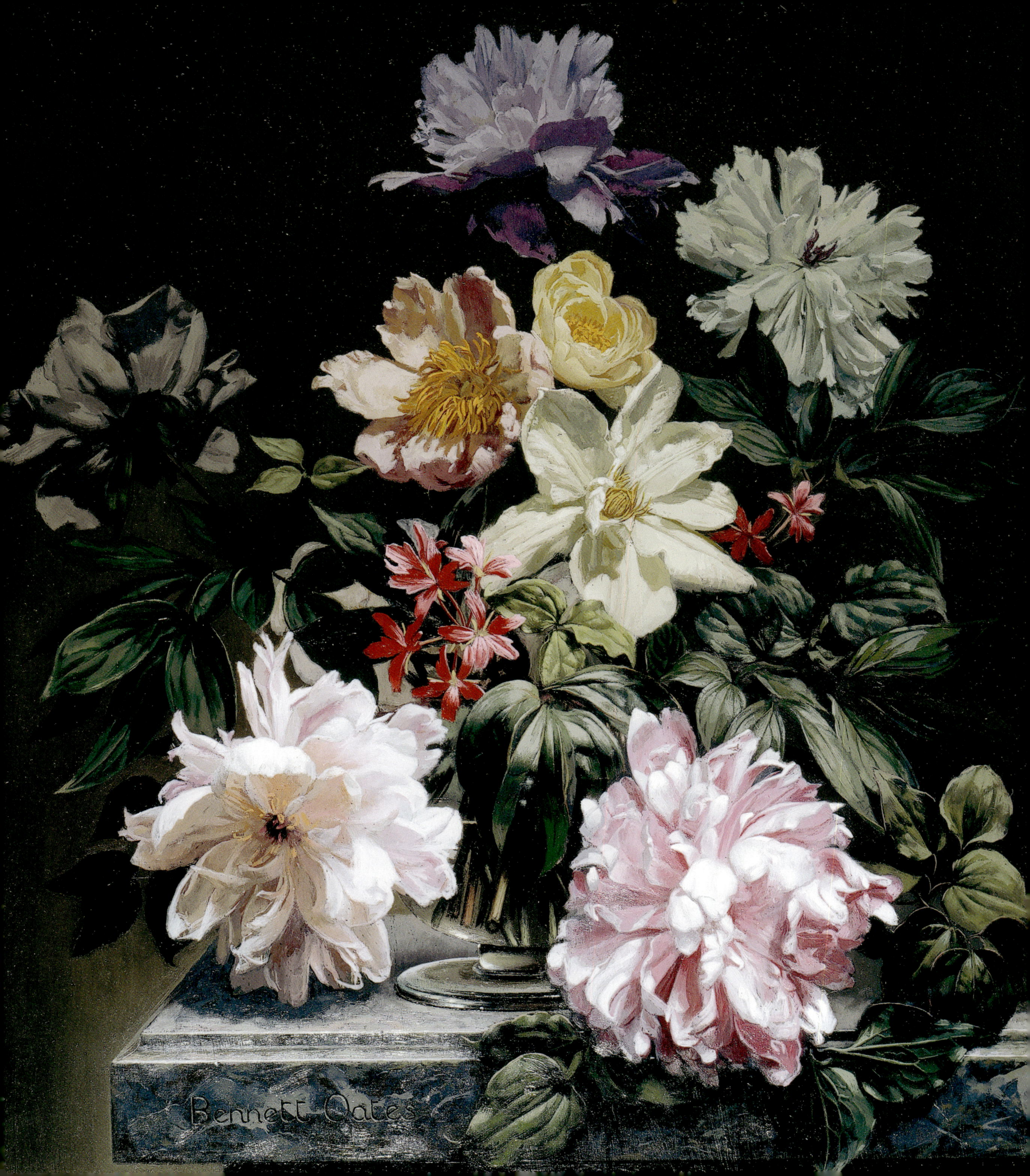
Bennett Oates

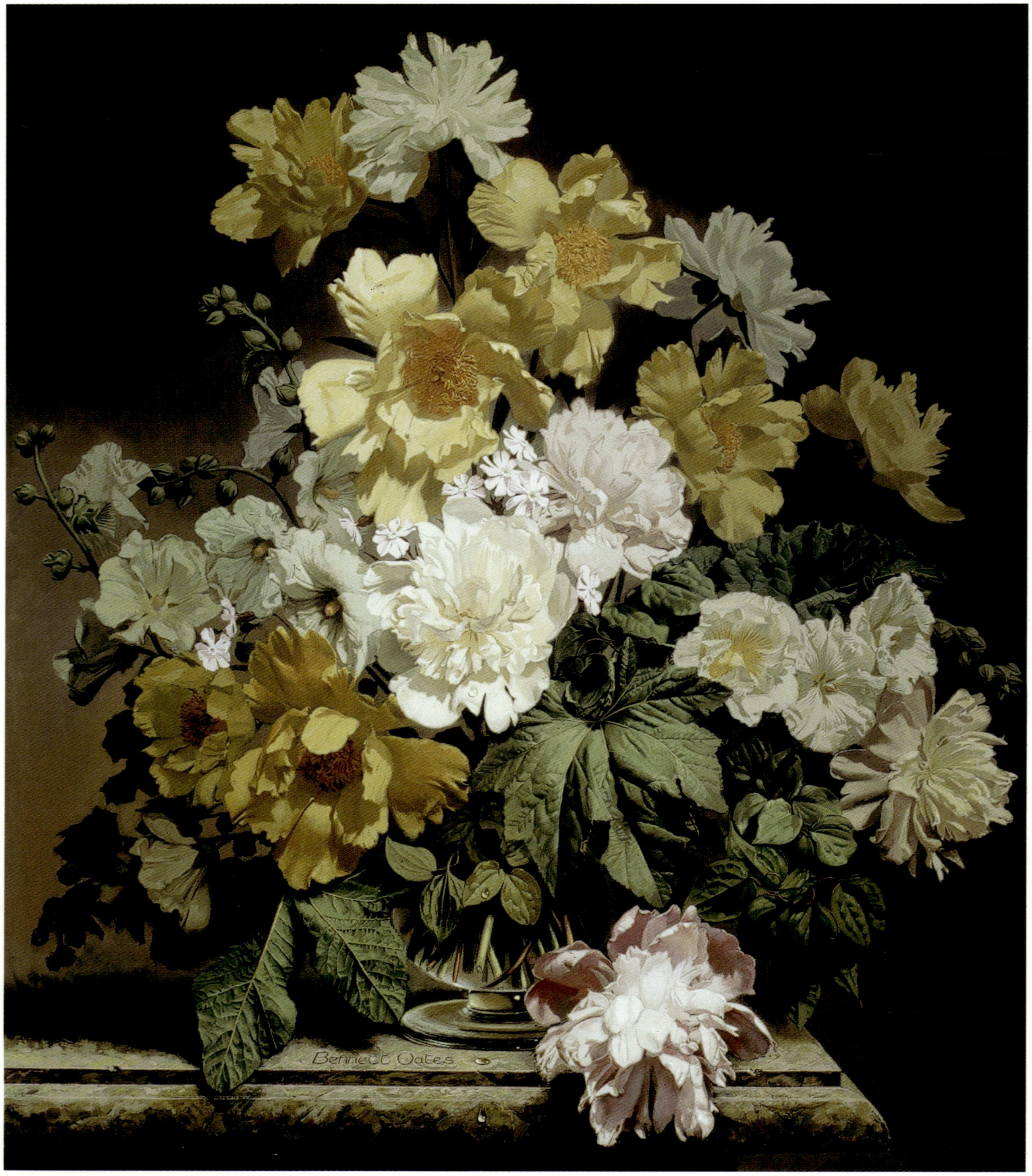
Bennett Oates

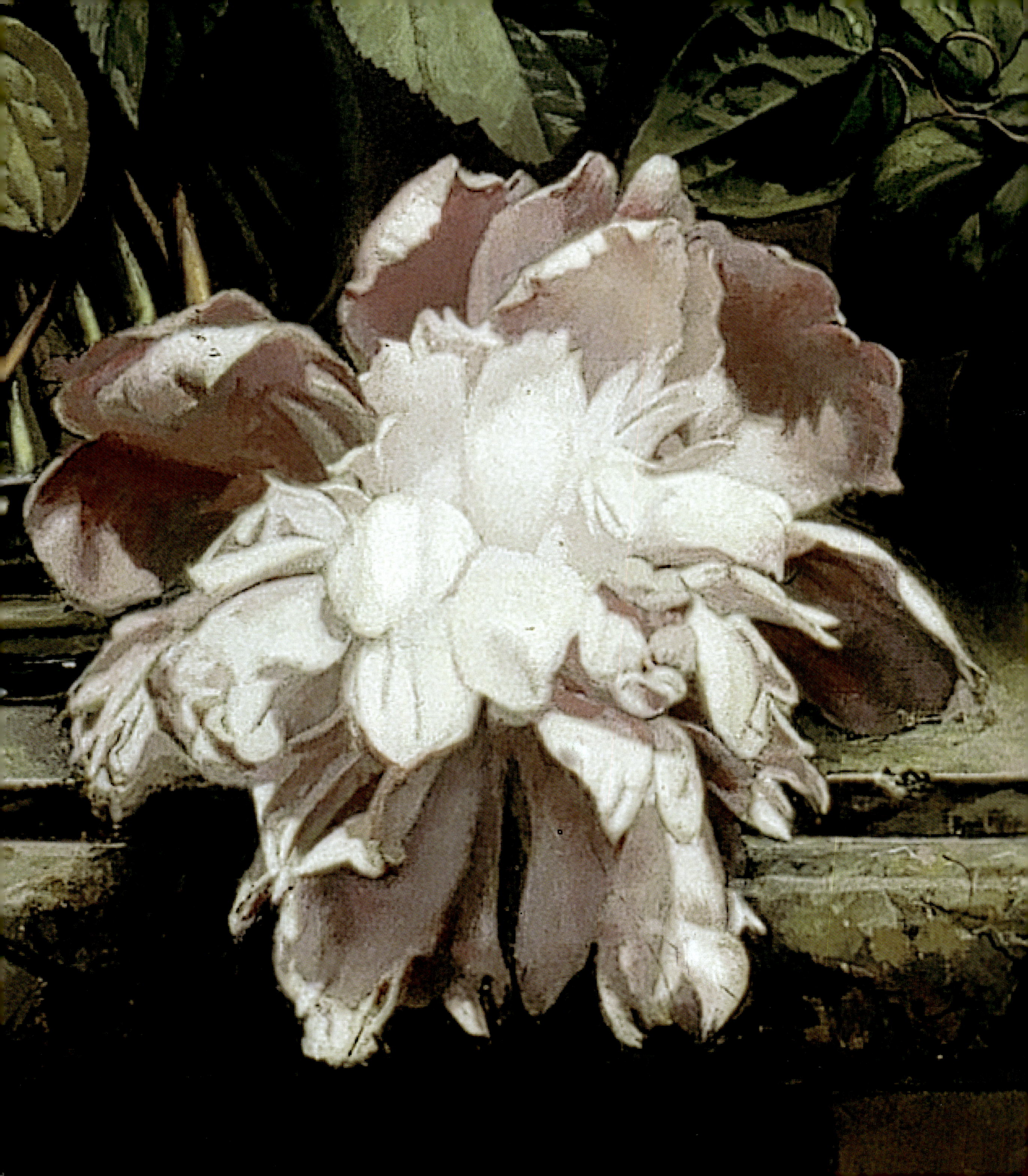

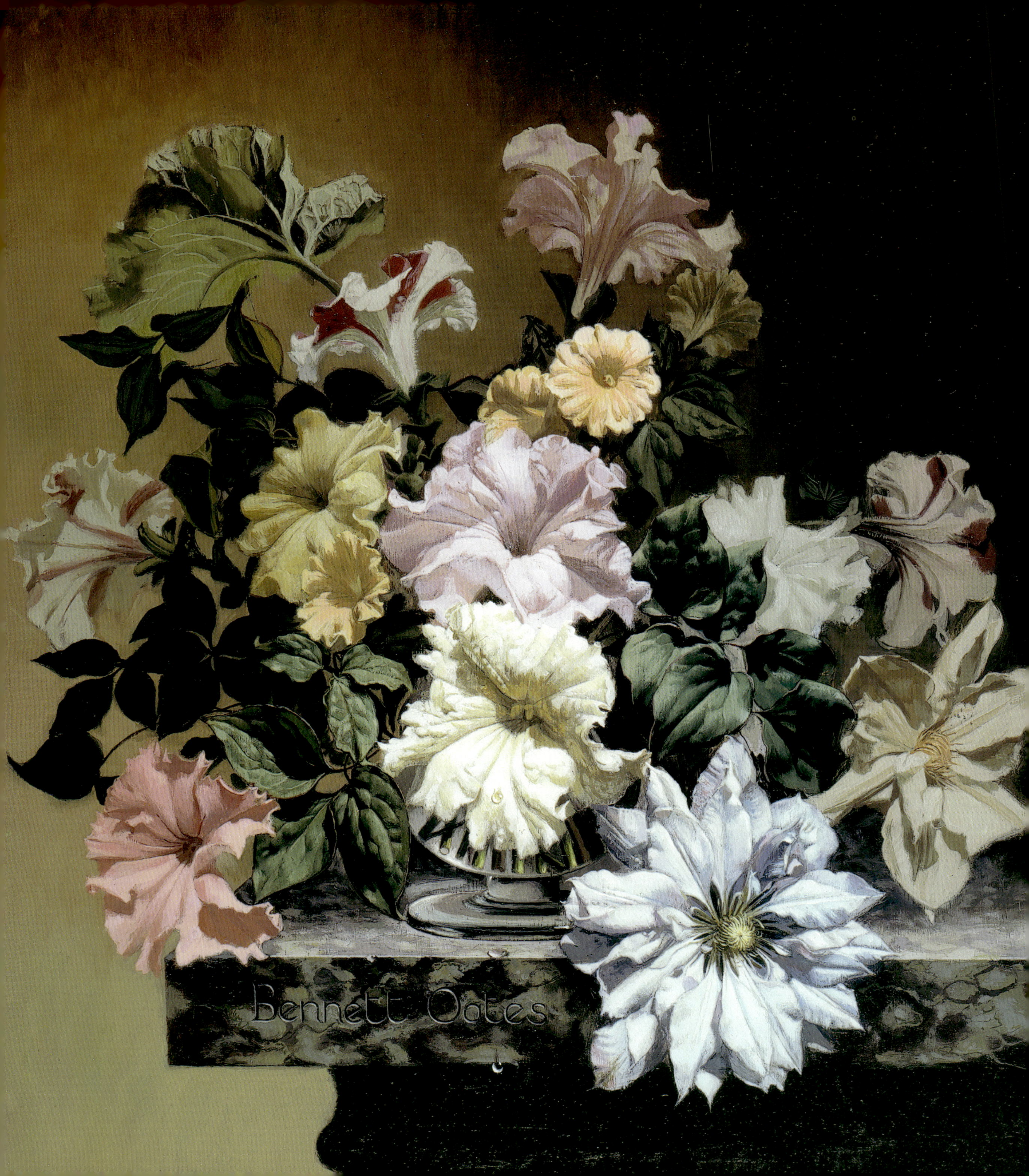
Bennett Oates

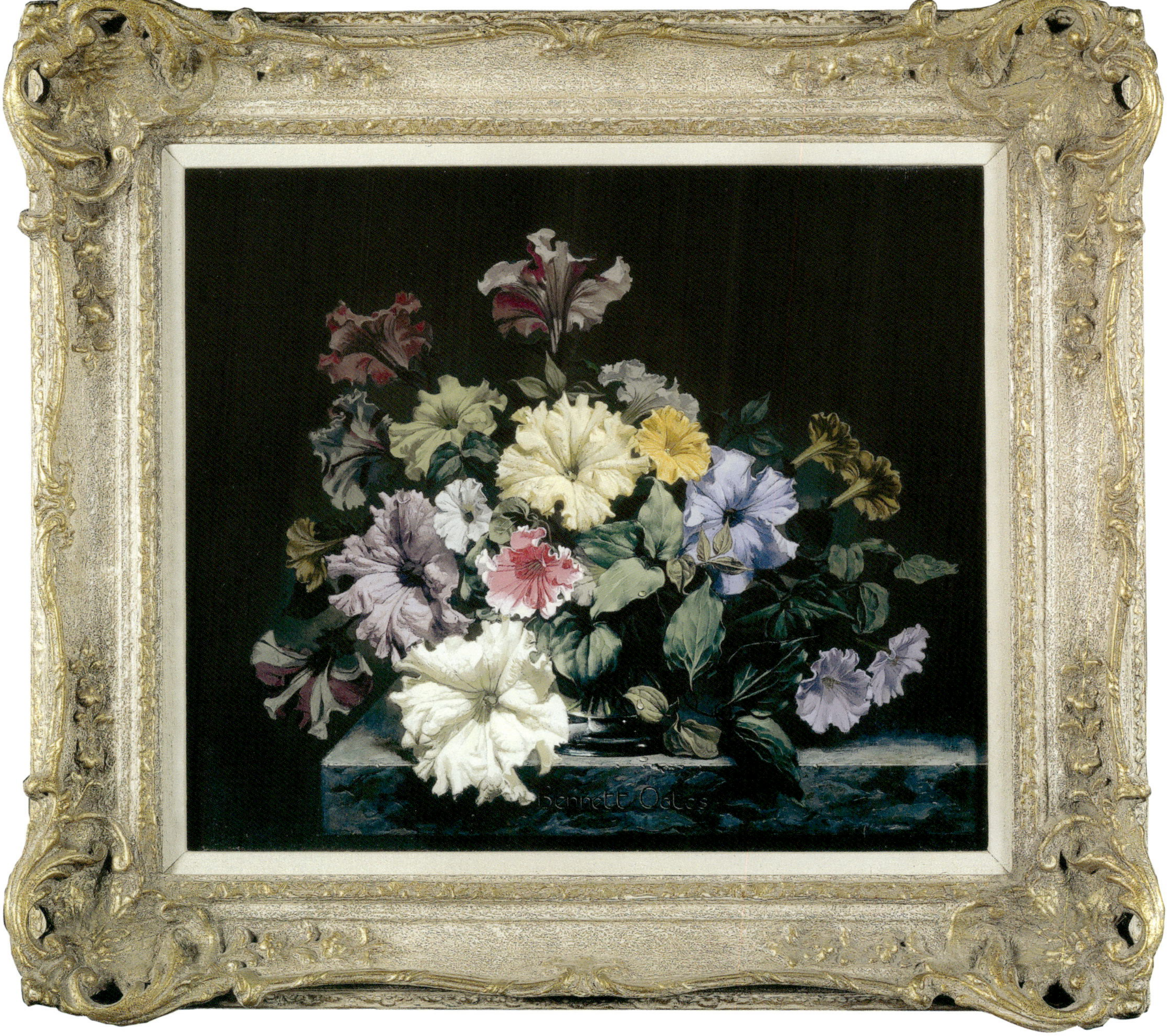
Bennett Oates

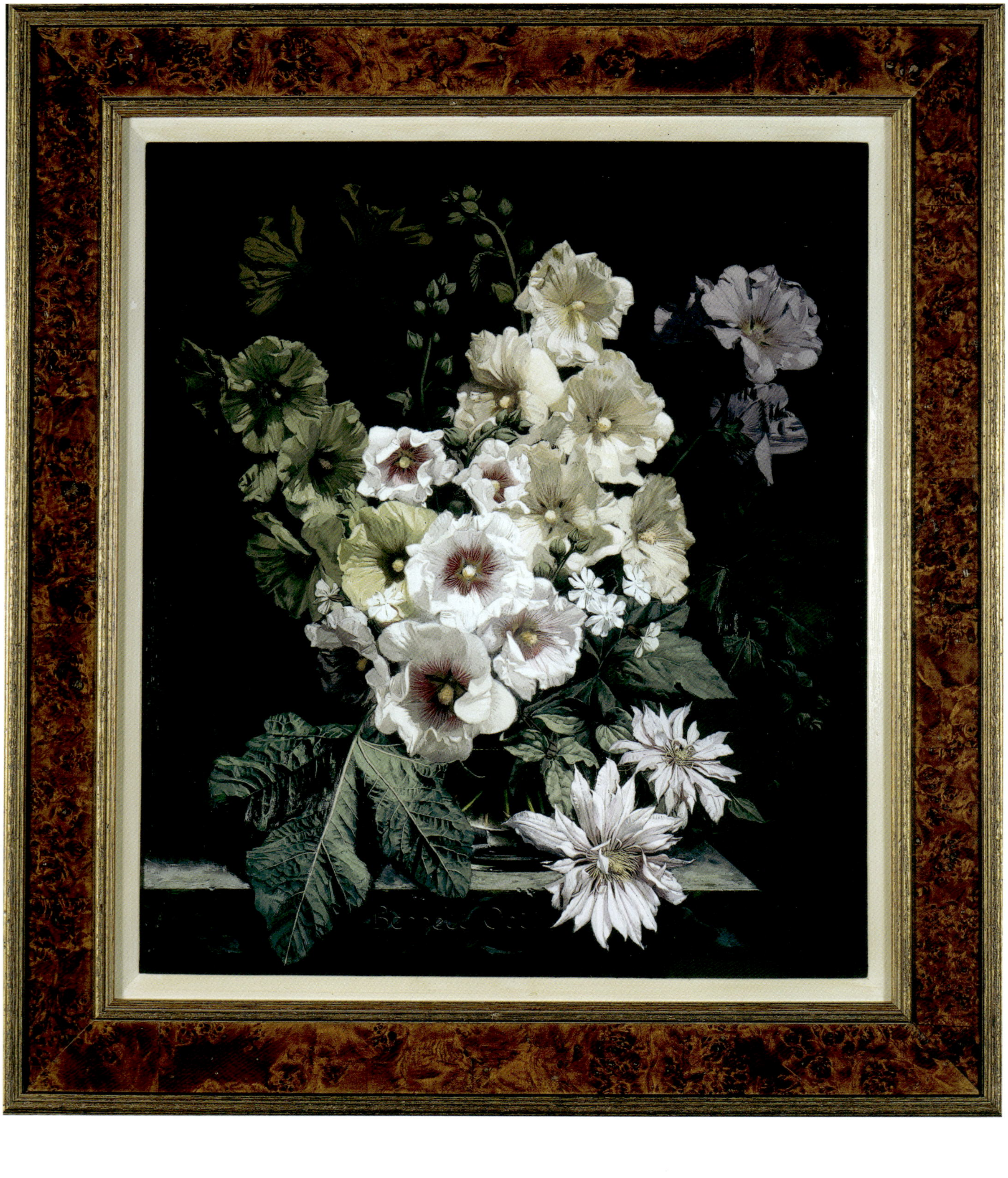

Flower-pieces dominated by modern, blue hybrids are a feature of Oates' work in later years. He has seized the opportunity offered by large blossoms from varieties of plants such as petunias, irises and clematis to explore the palette in spectacular ways that were not open to his predecessors. Thus Oates has made a distinctive contribution to the development of the distinguished and demanding tradition of flower painting.

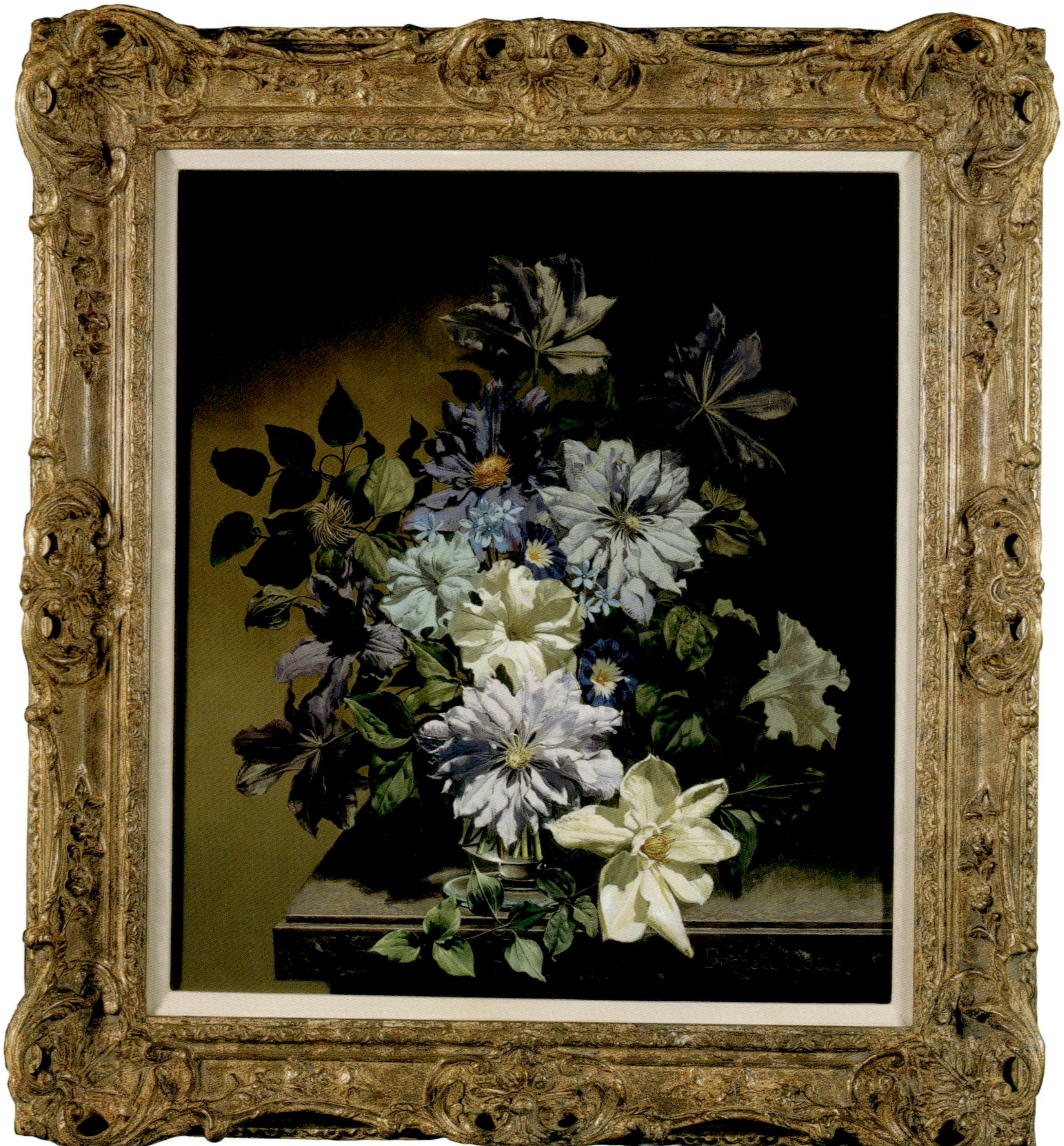

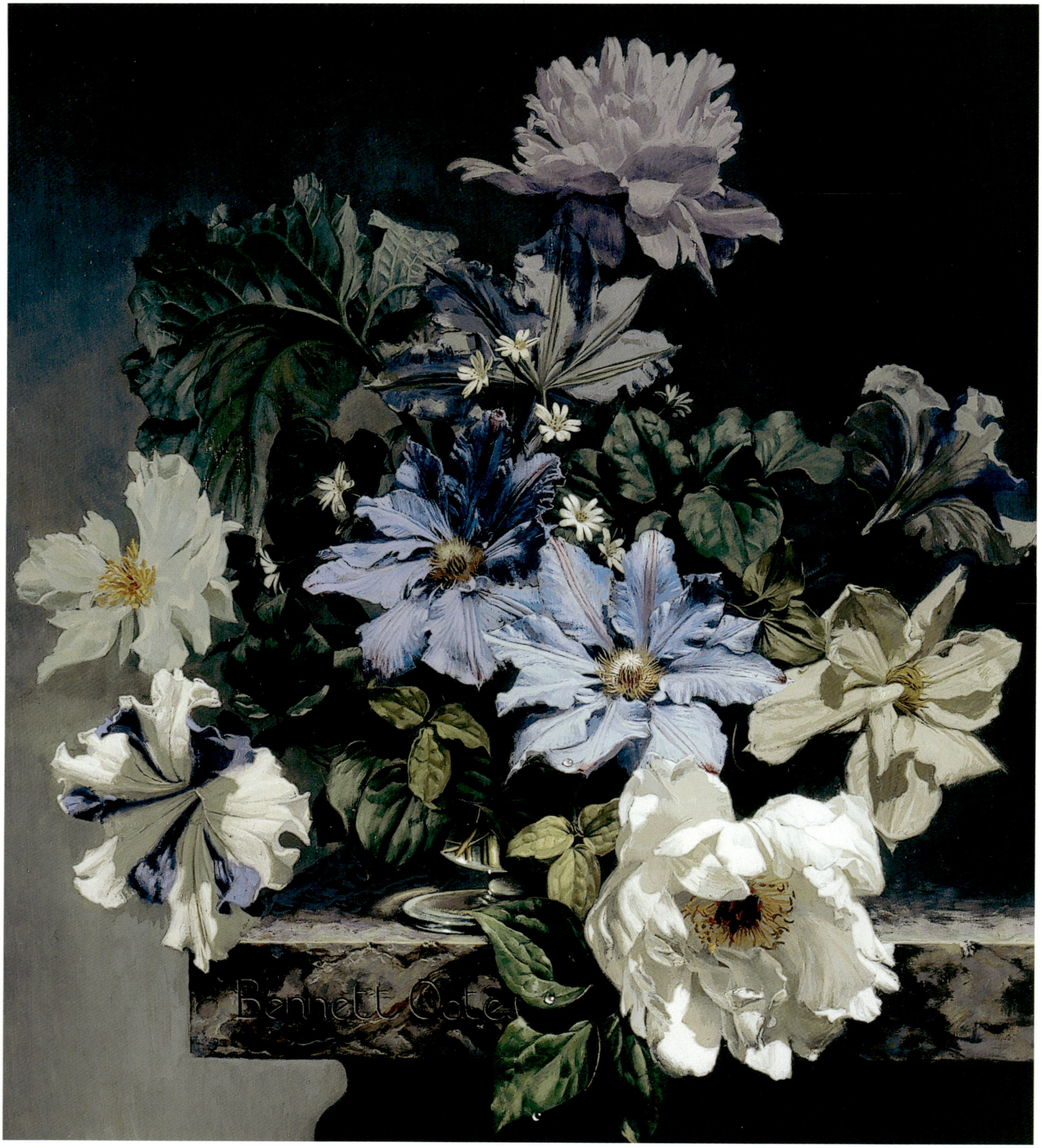
Bennett Oate

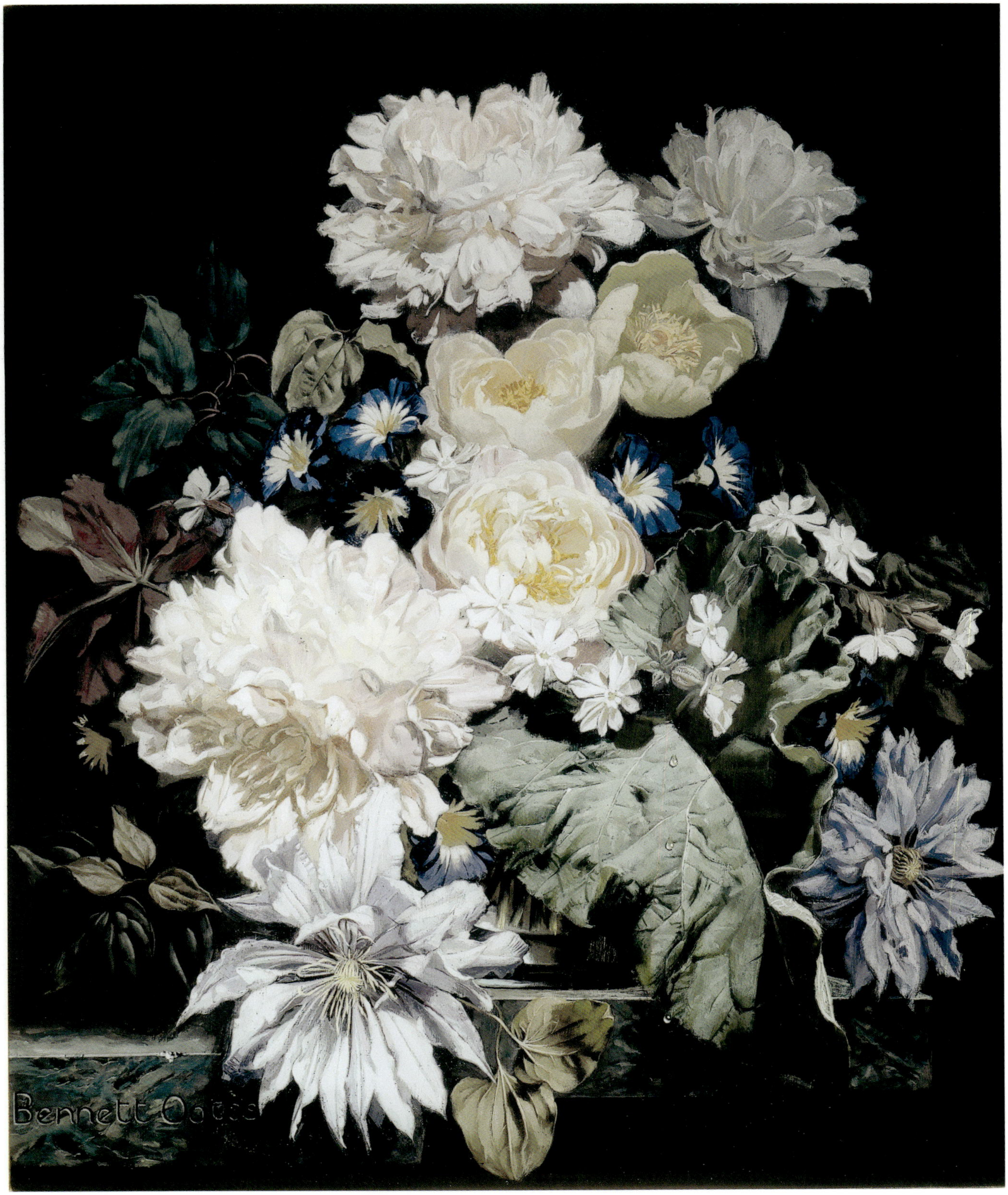
Bennett Oates

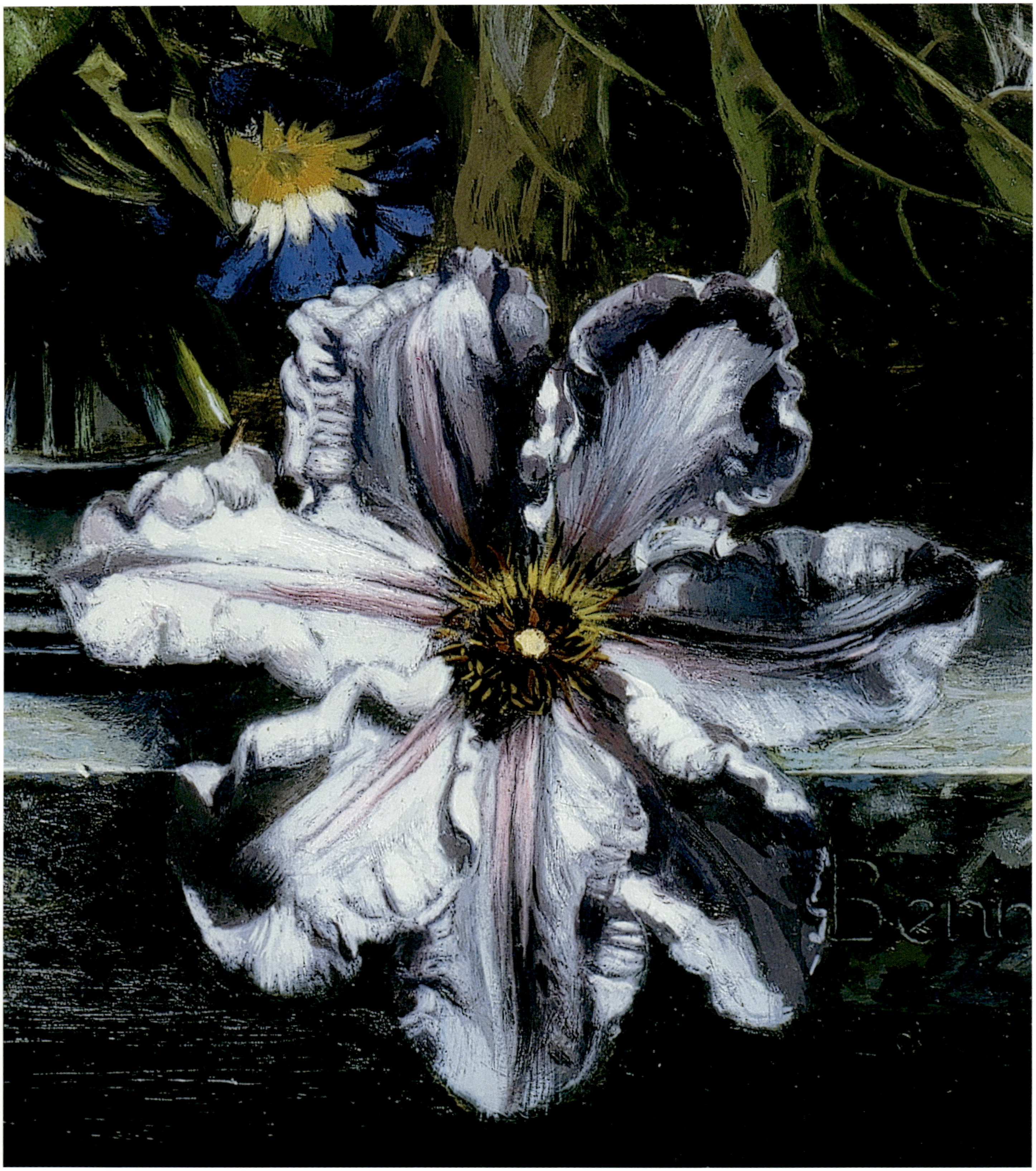

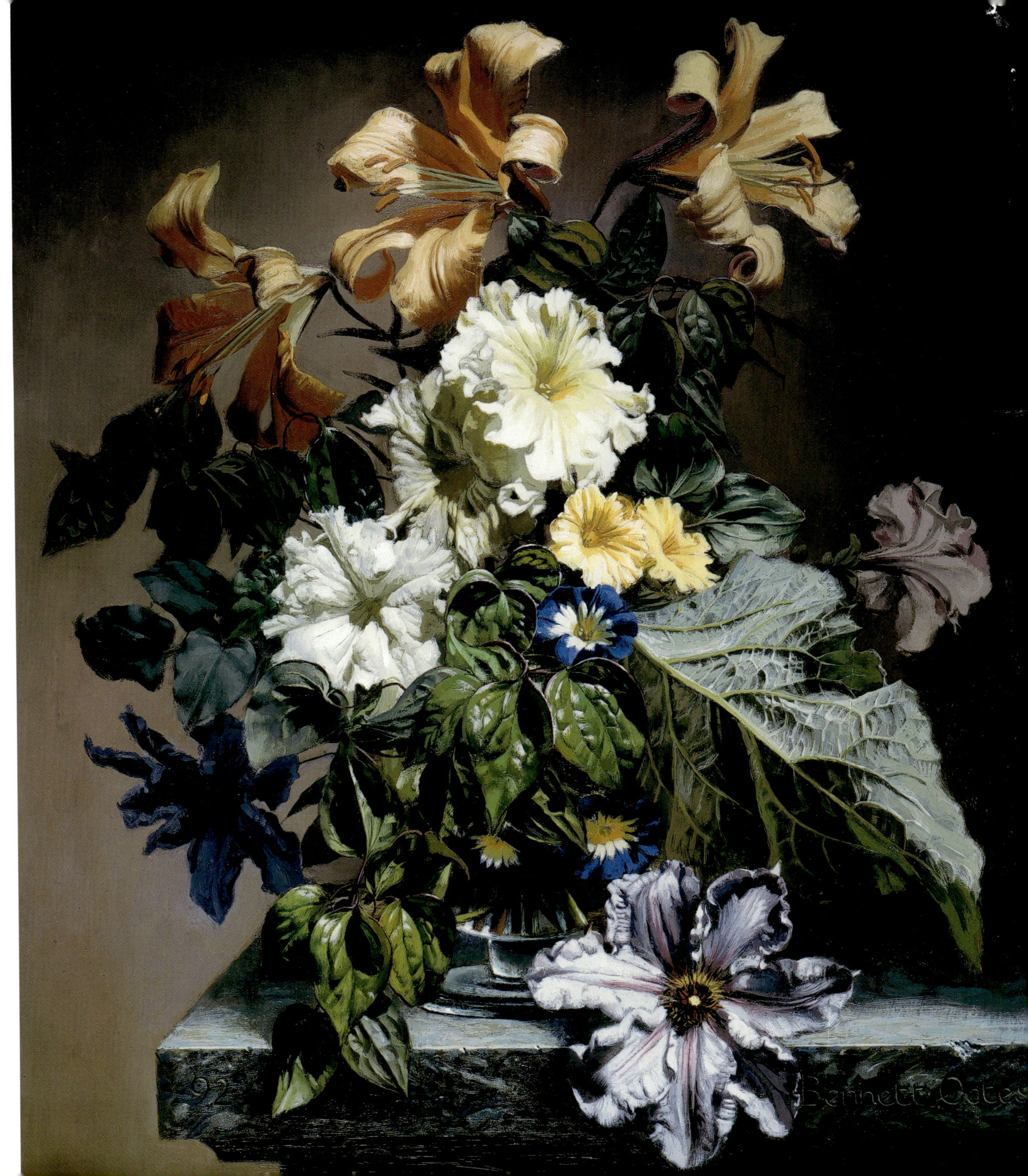

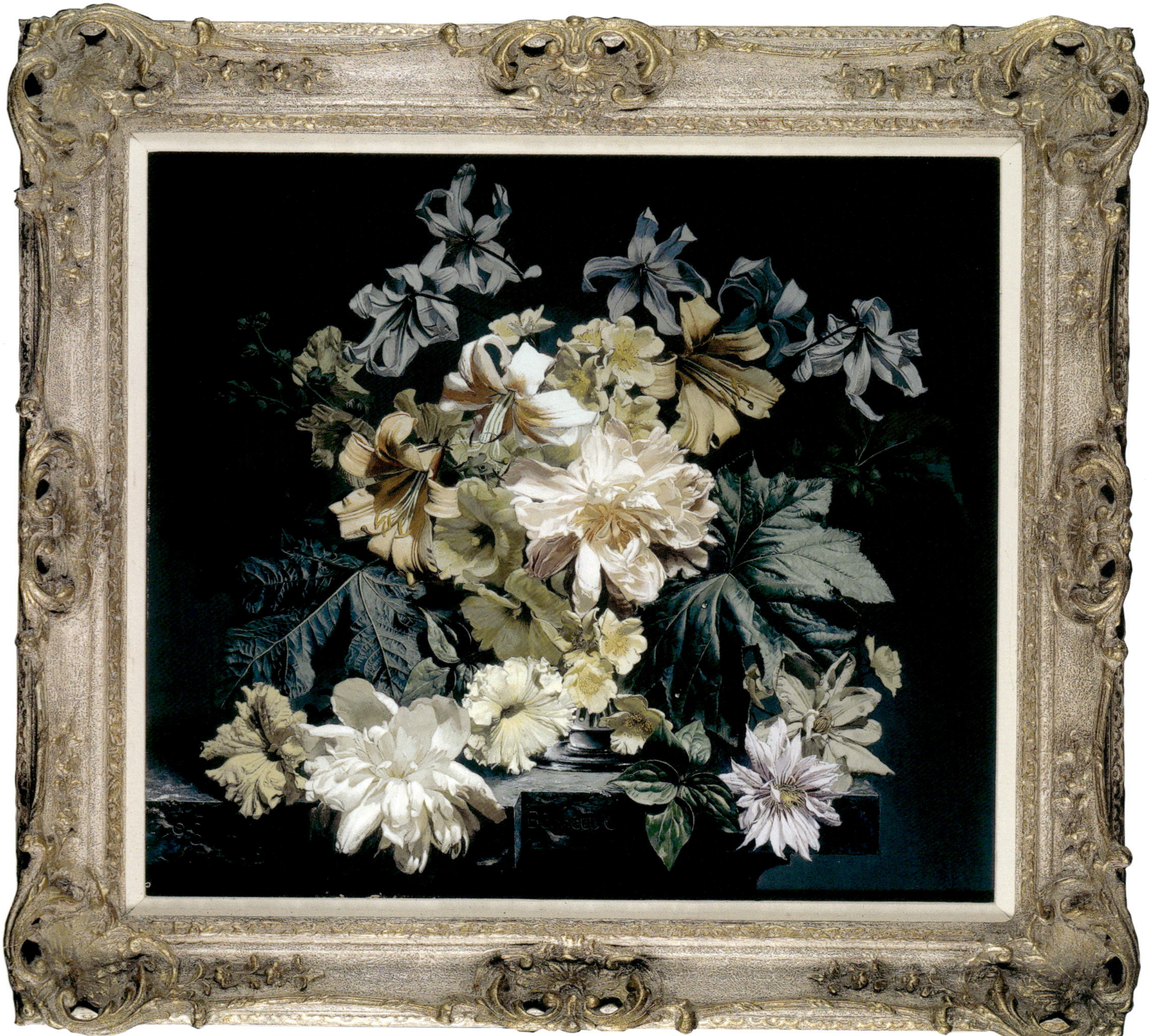

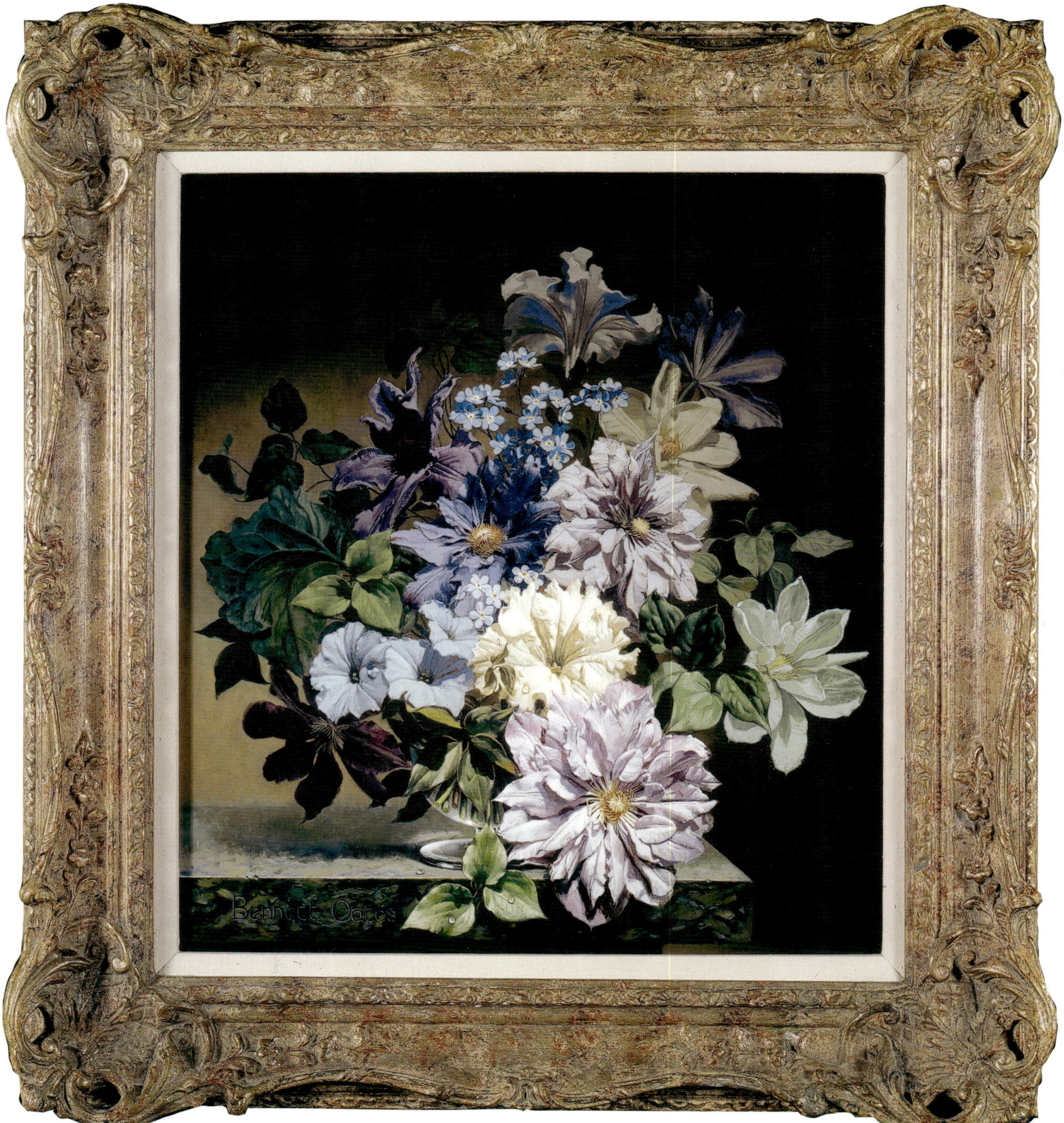
Bennett Oates

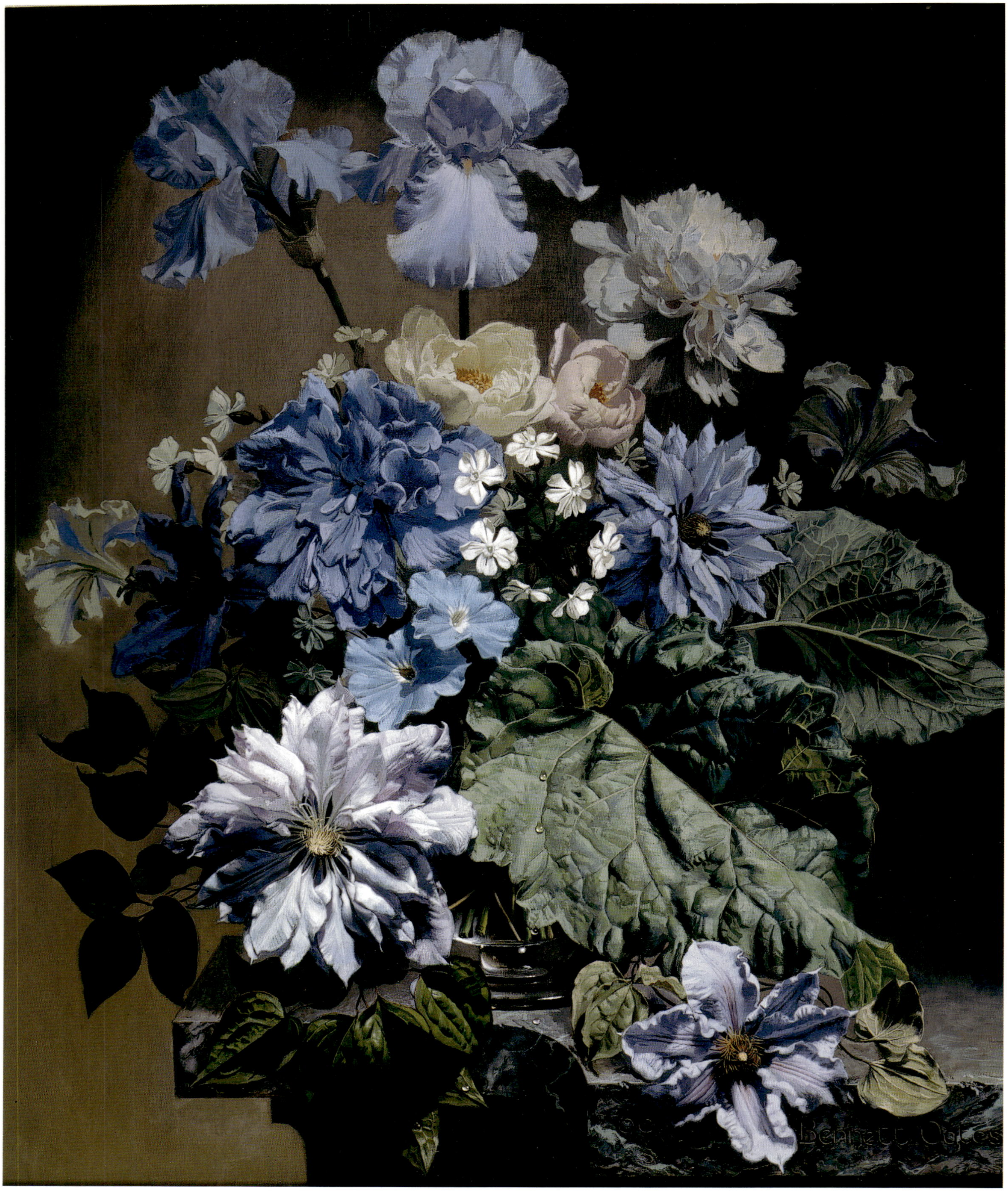
Bennett Oates

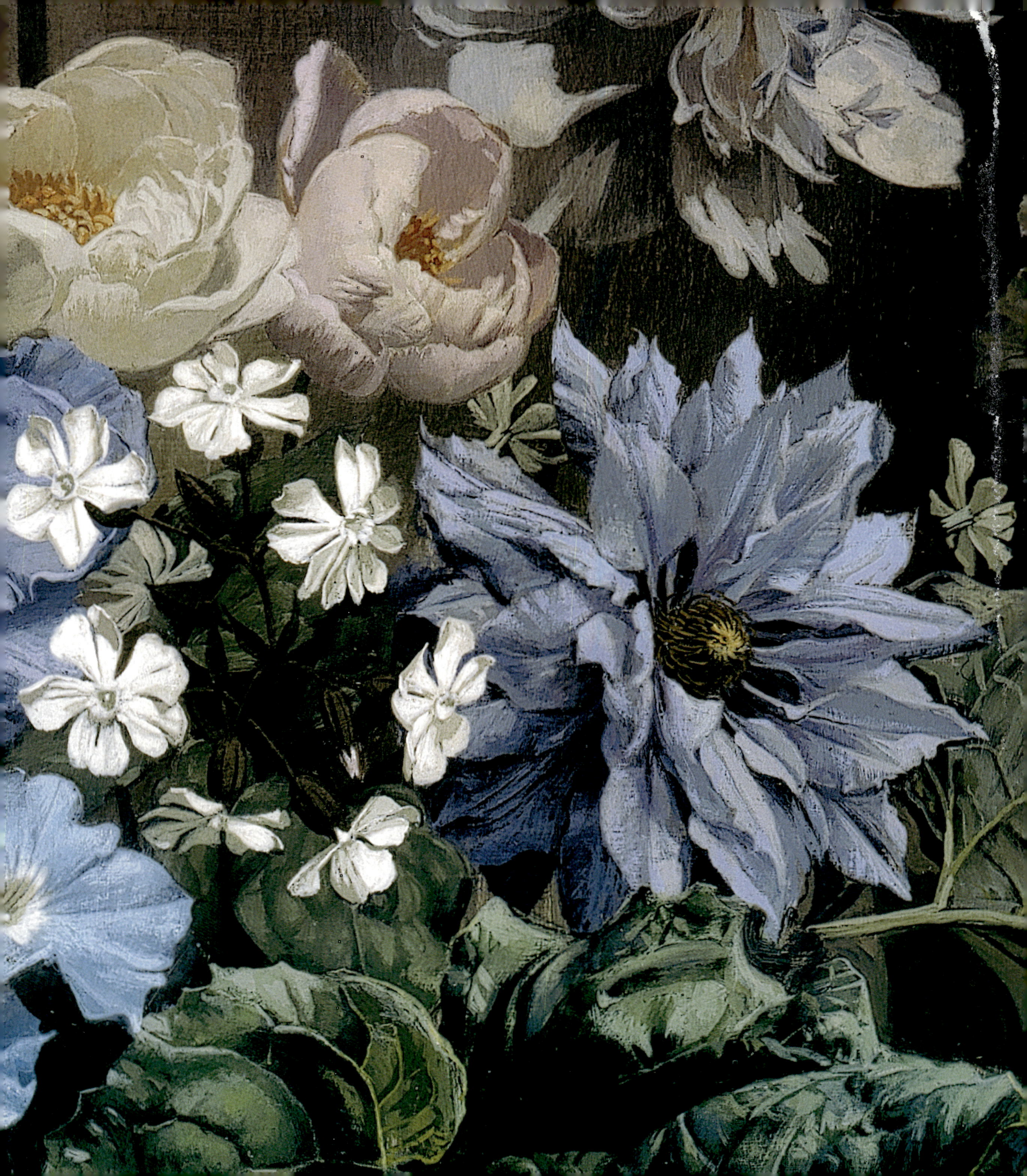

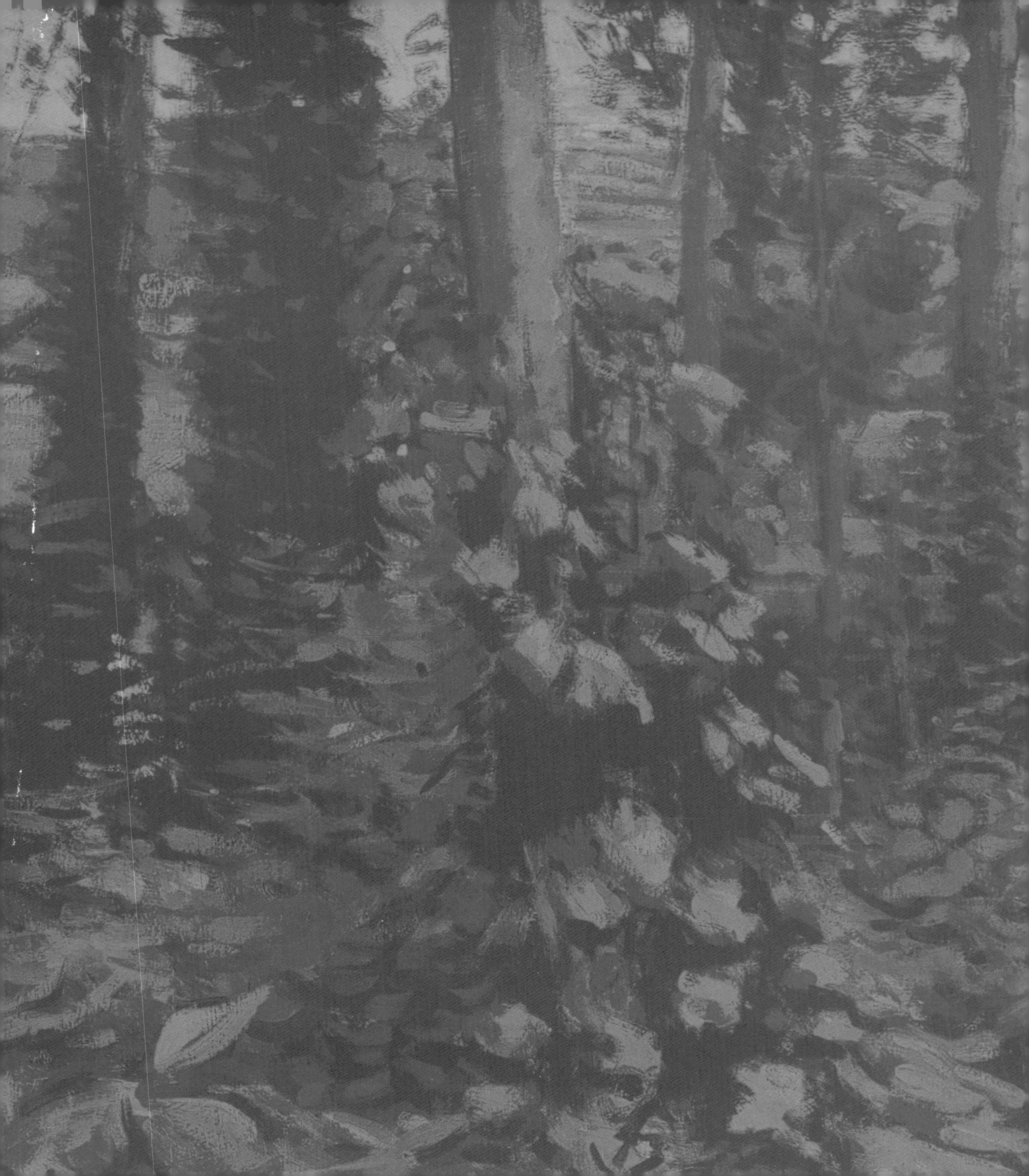

LANDSCAPES

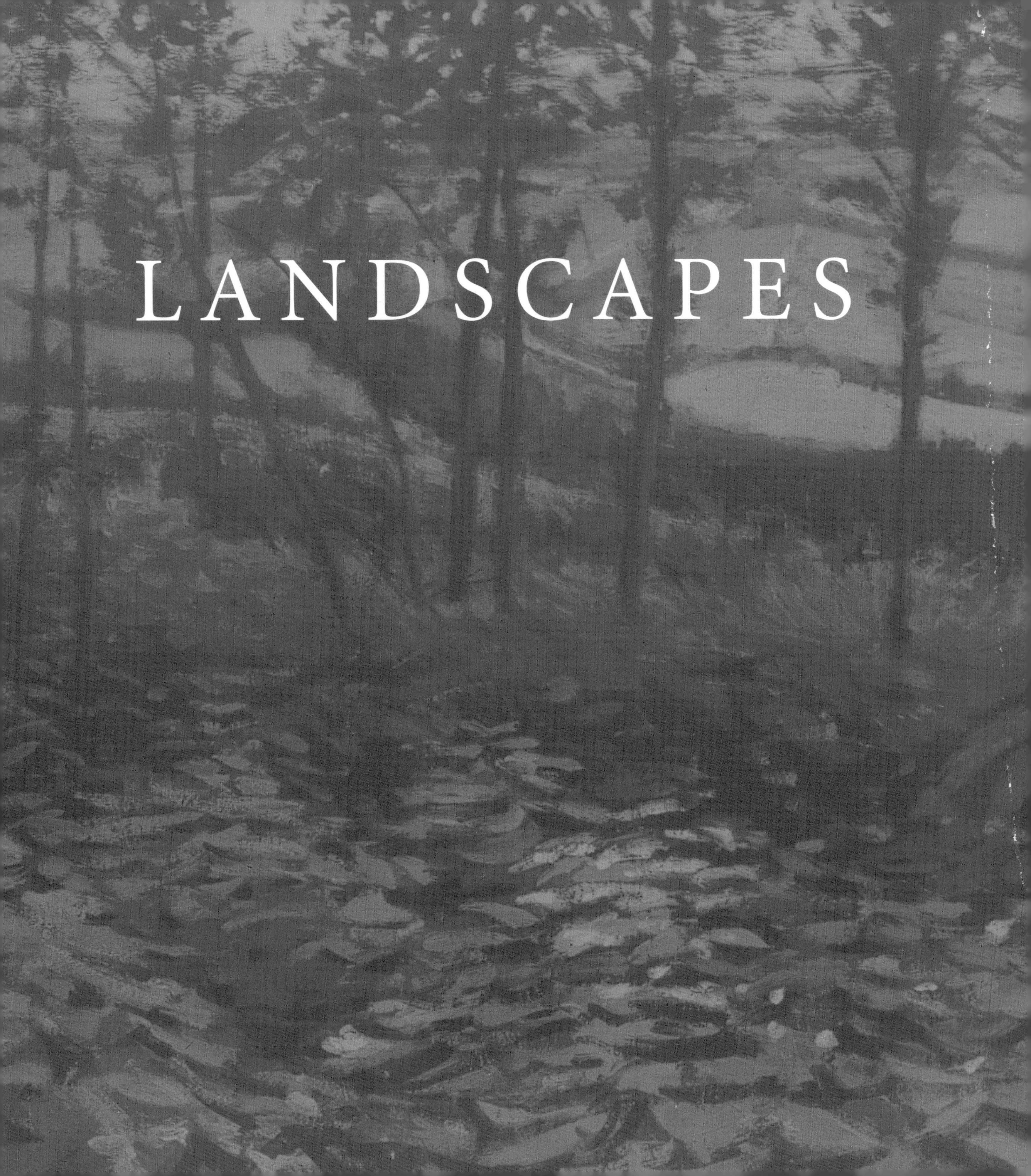

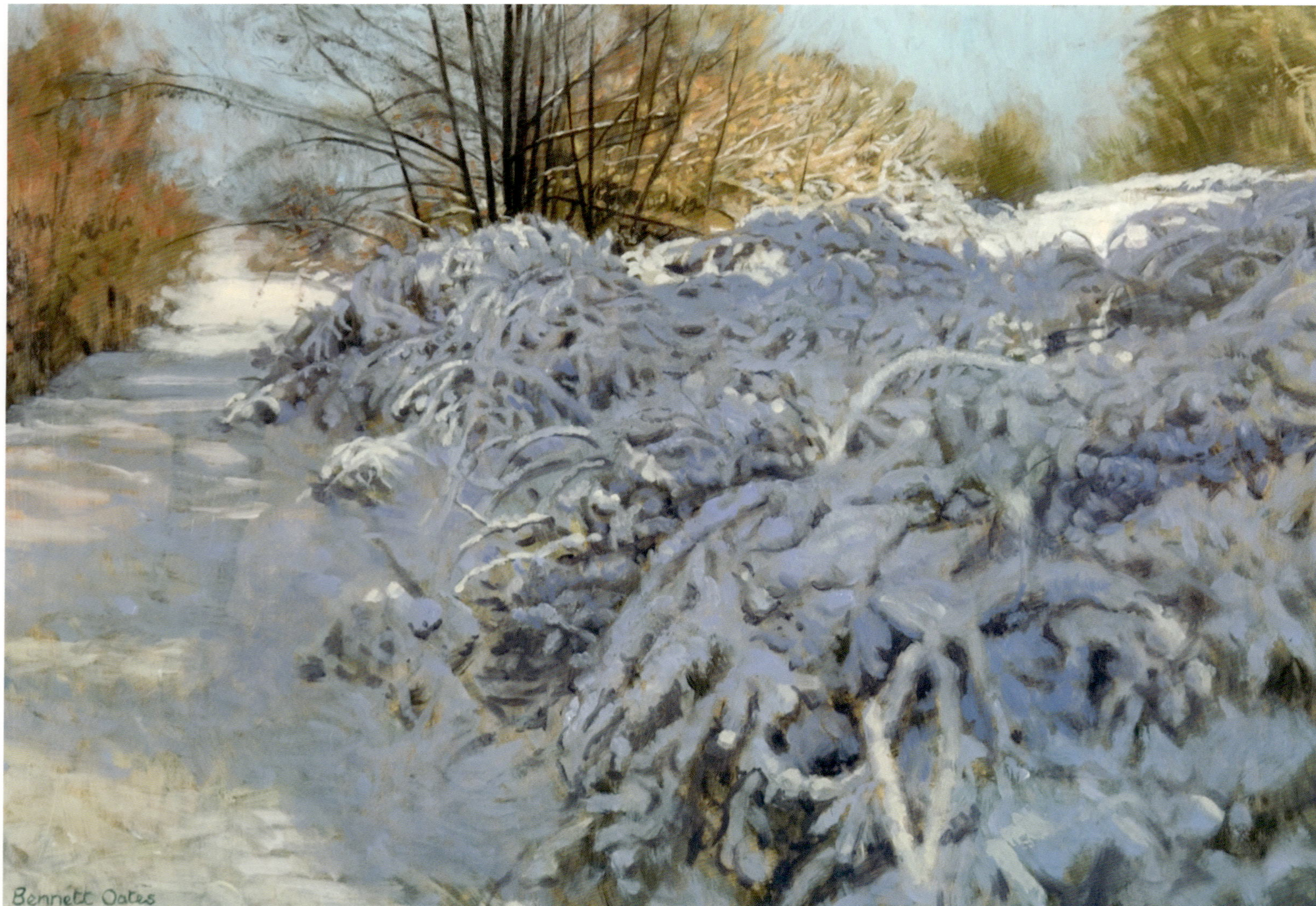

SNOW ON BRAMBLES

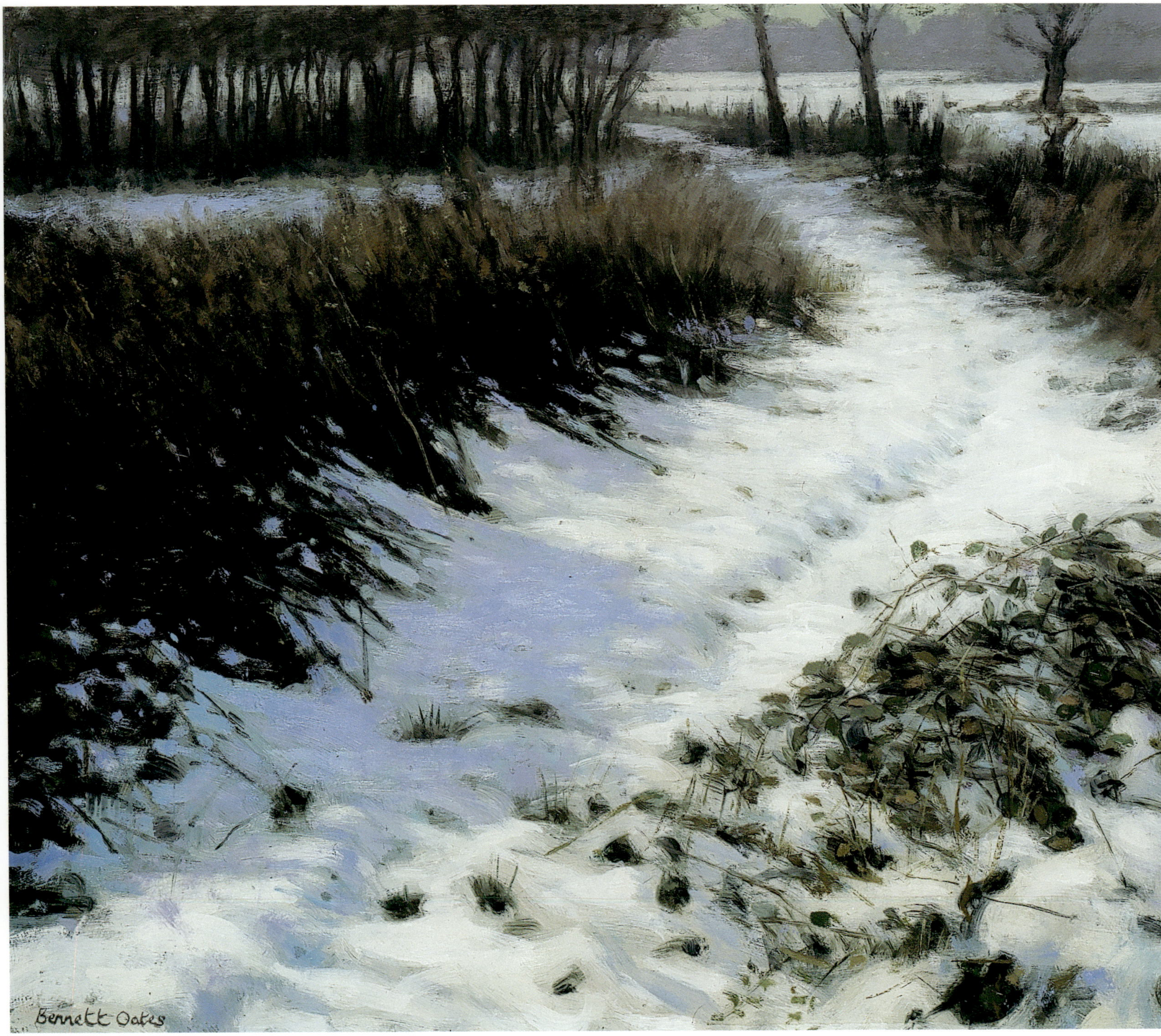

WINTER LANDSCAPE

BONFIRE

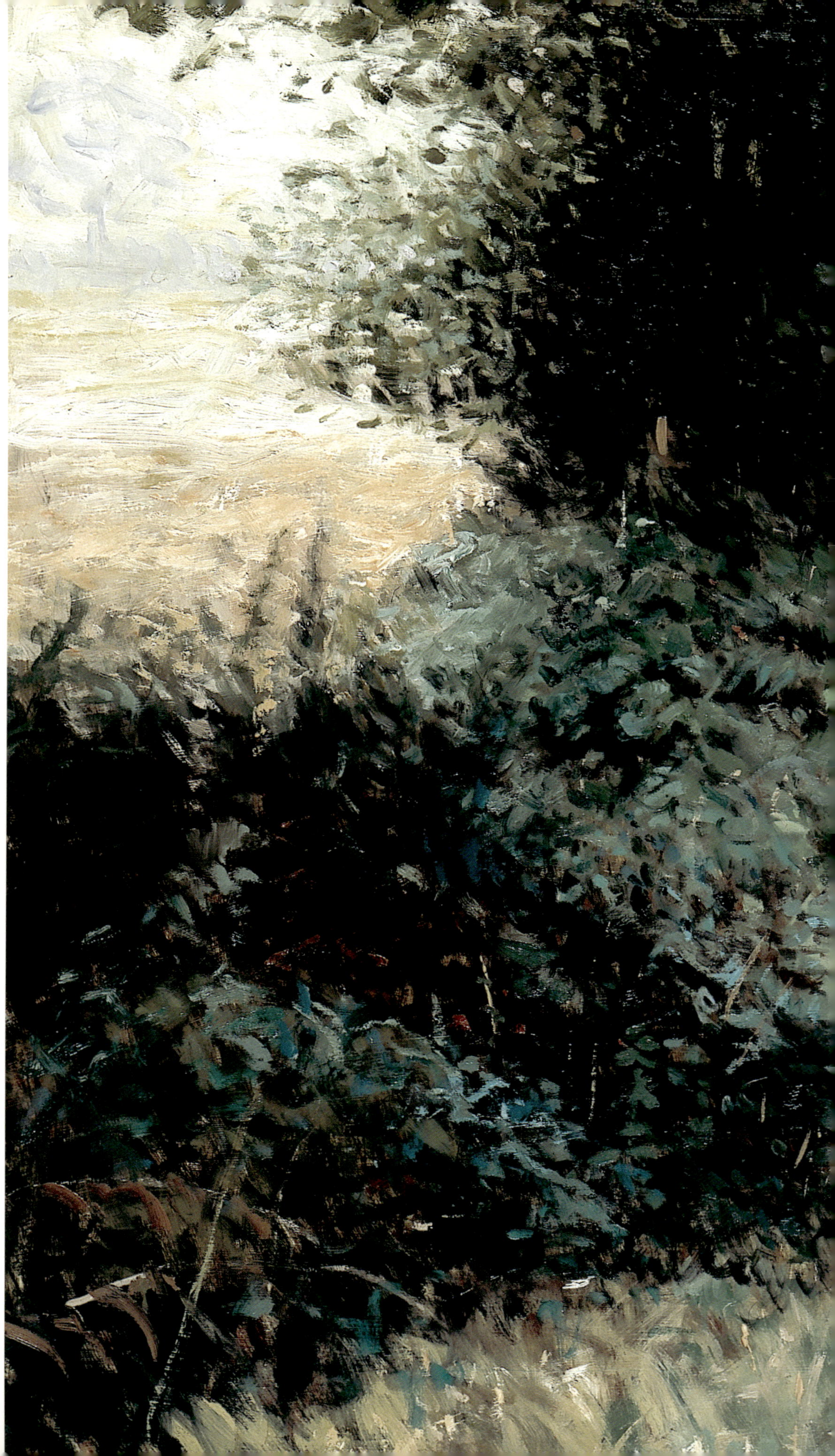

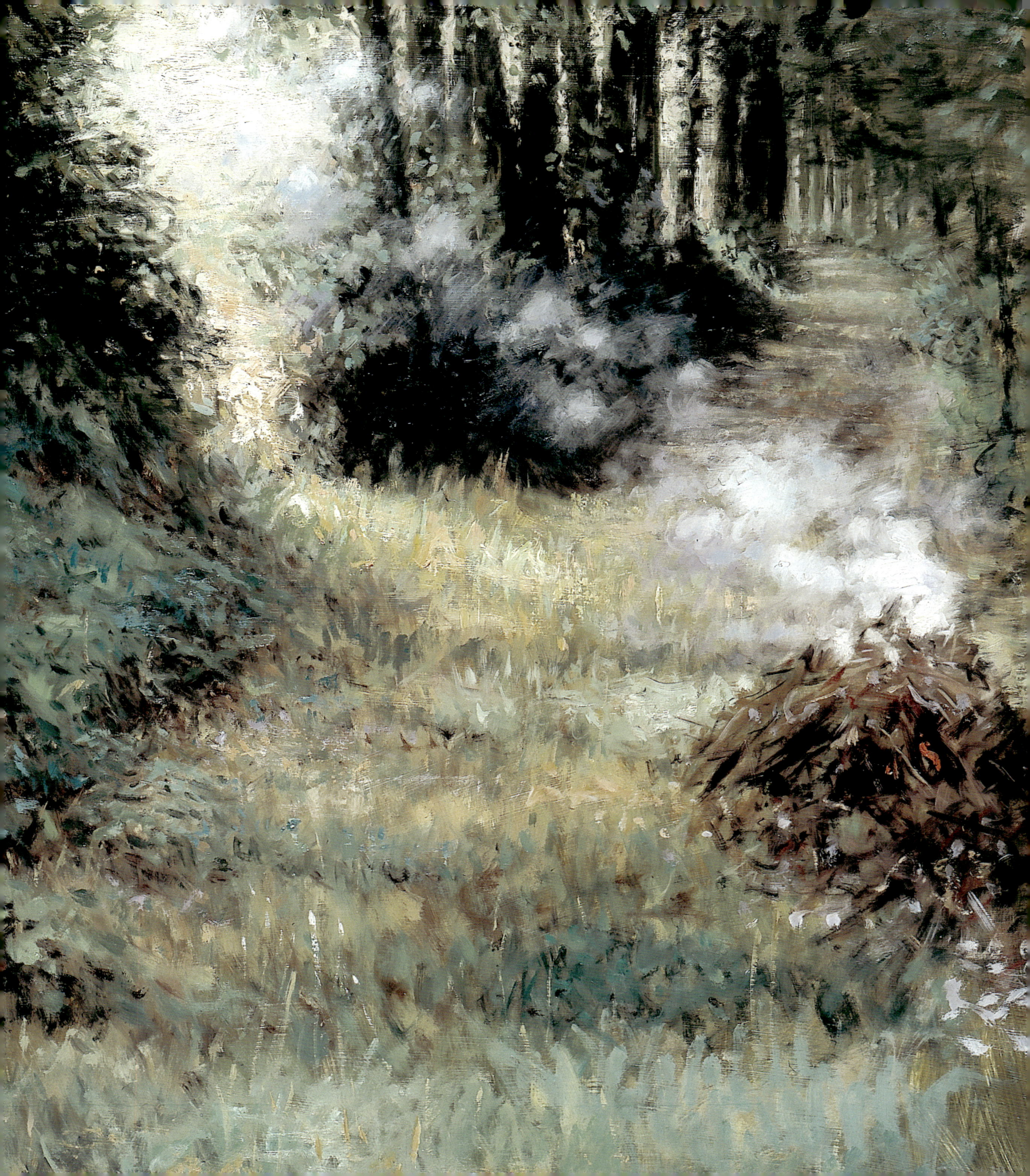

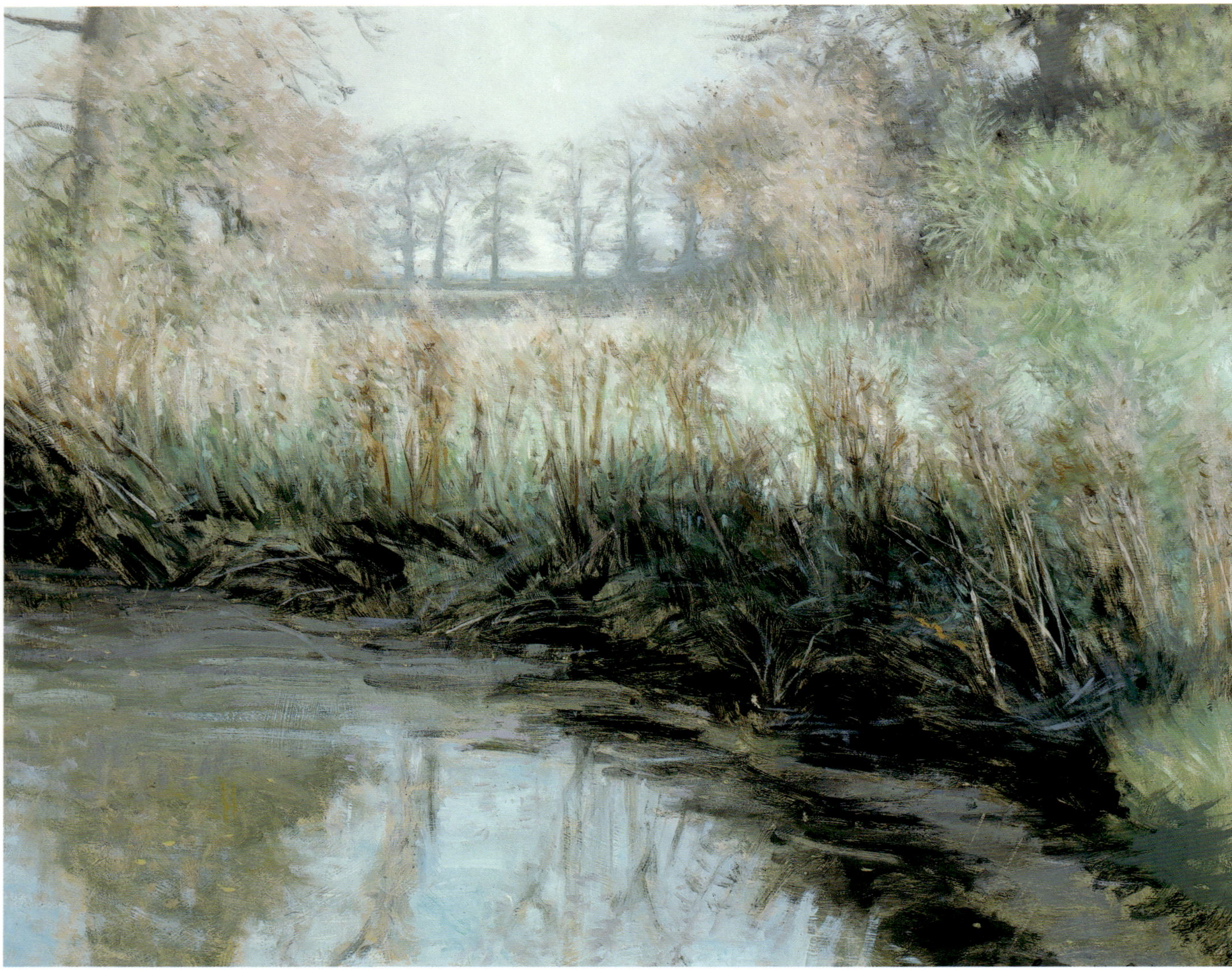

MISTY MORNING

GREENWOOD

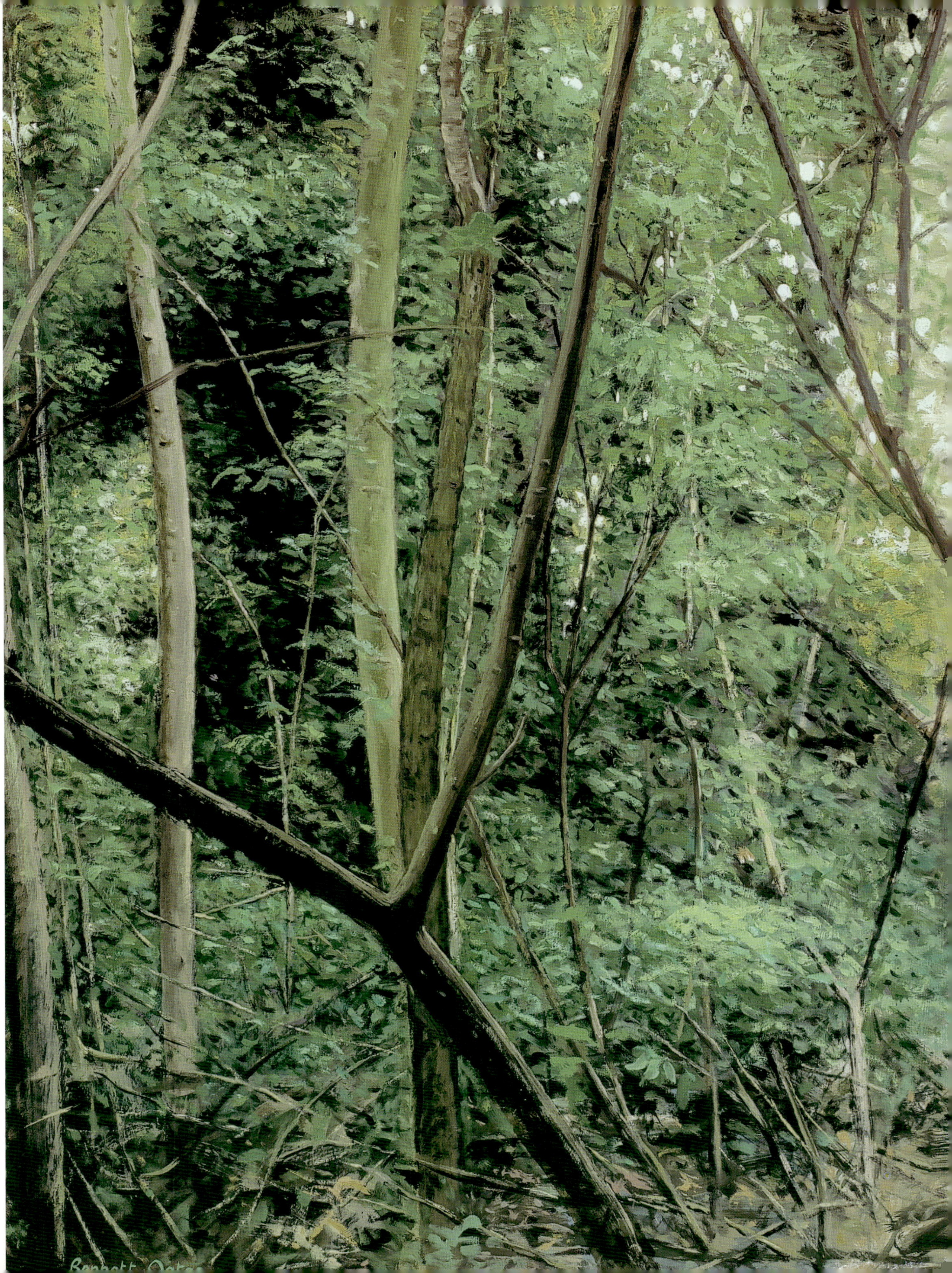

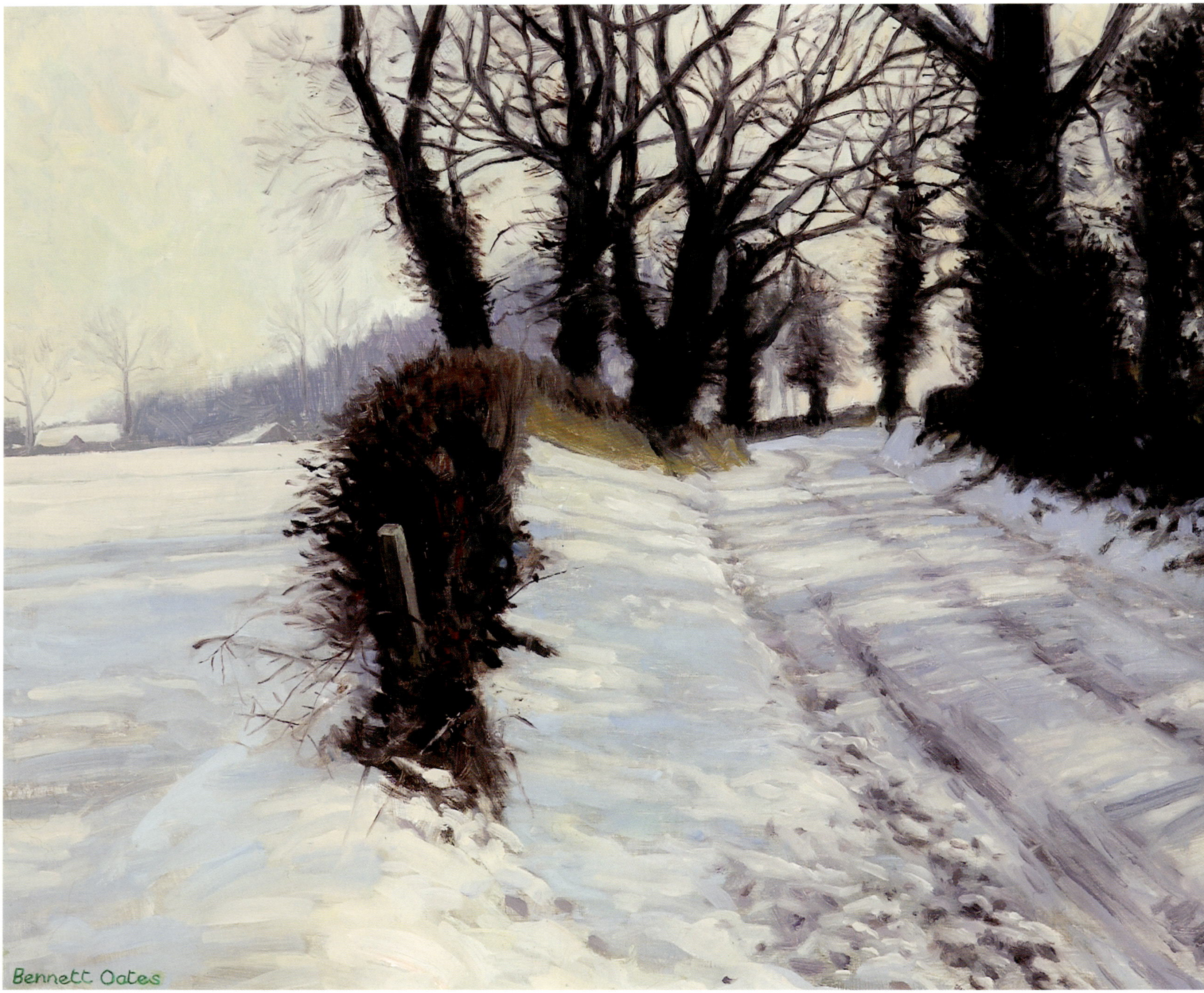

SNOW, LITTLE PLUMSTEAD

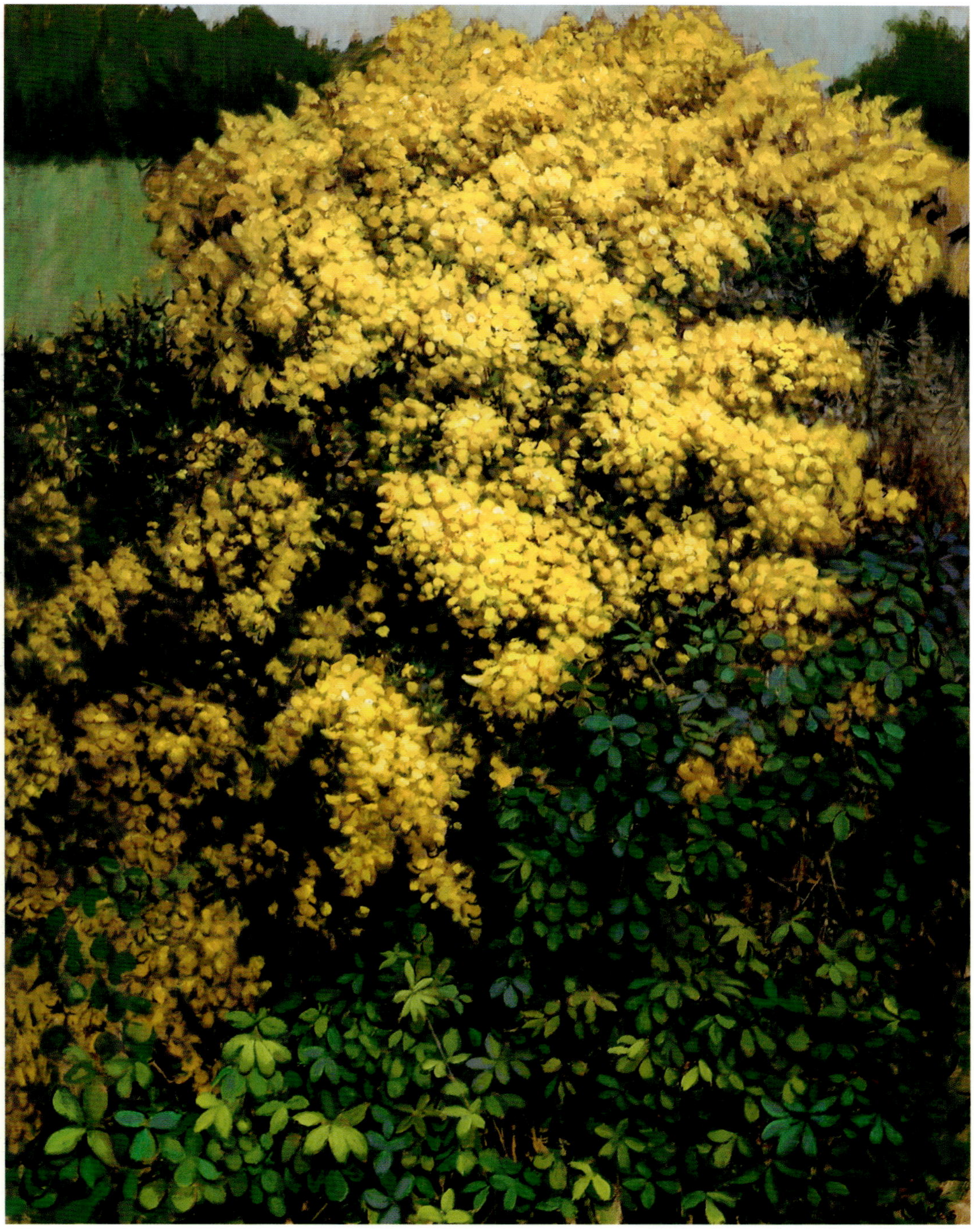

ANALYSIS OF A GORSE BUSH

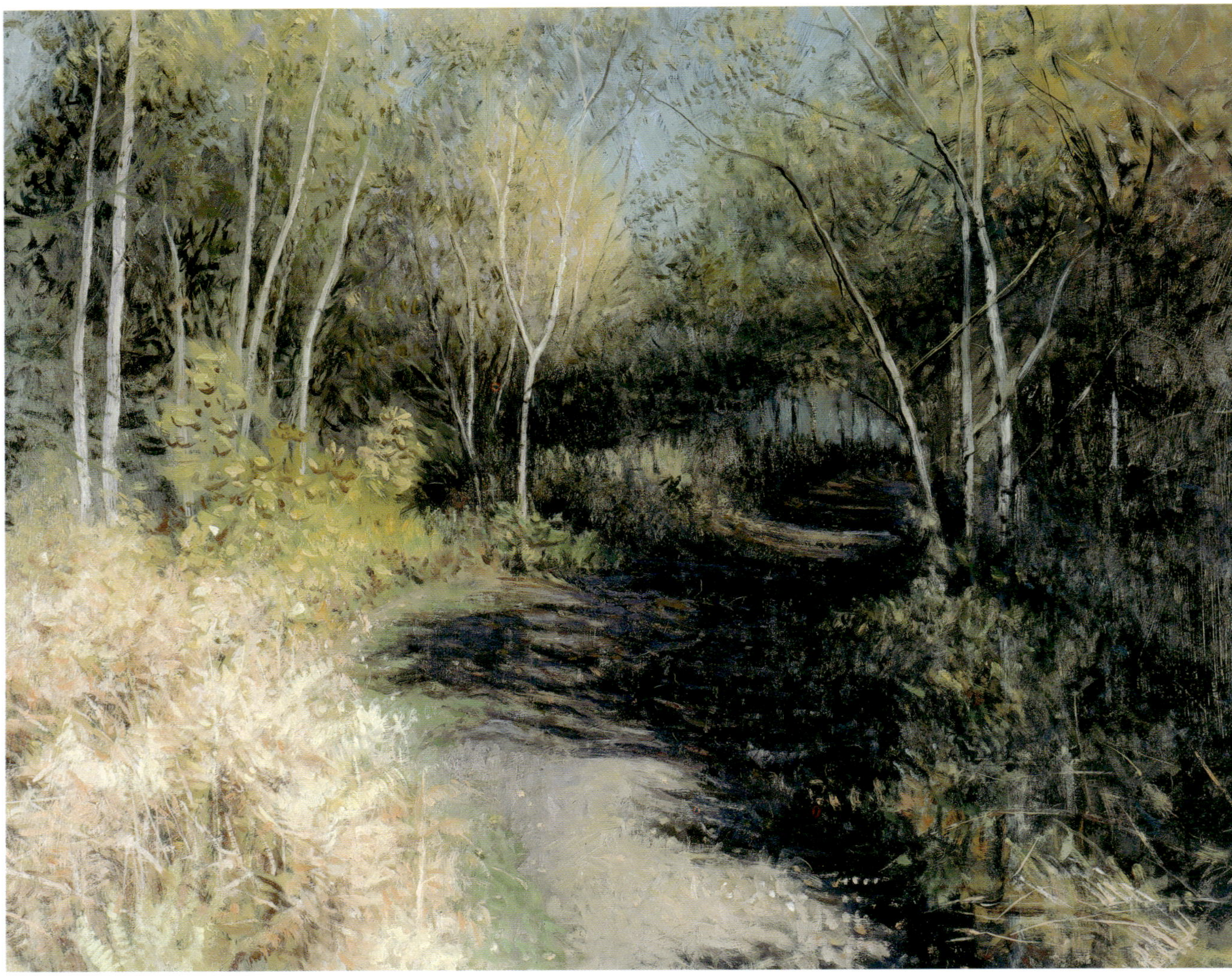

MOUSEHOLD HEATH, NORWICH

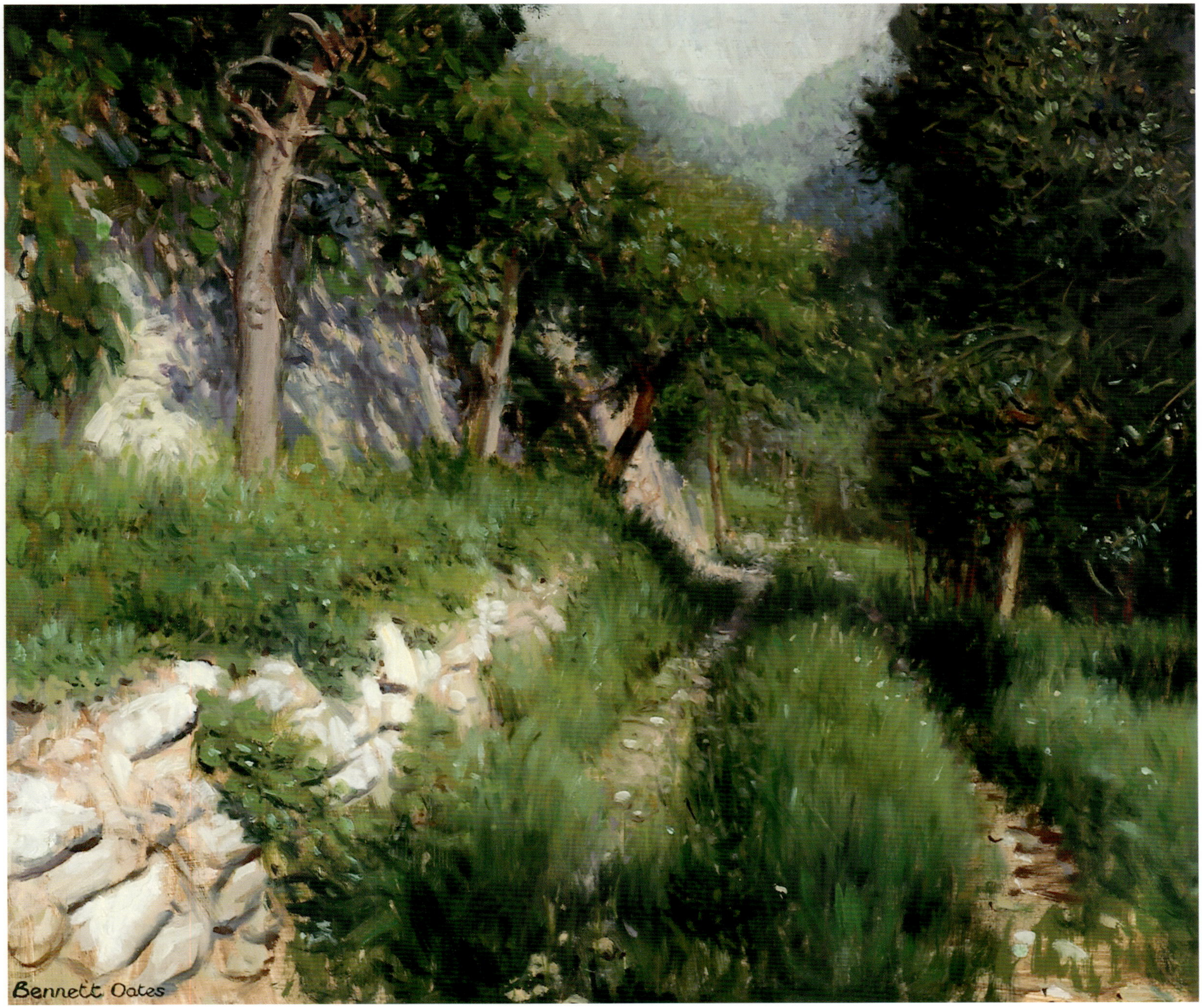

FARM TRACK, TUSCANY

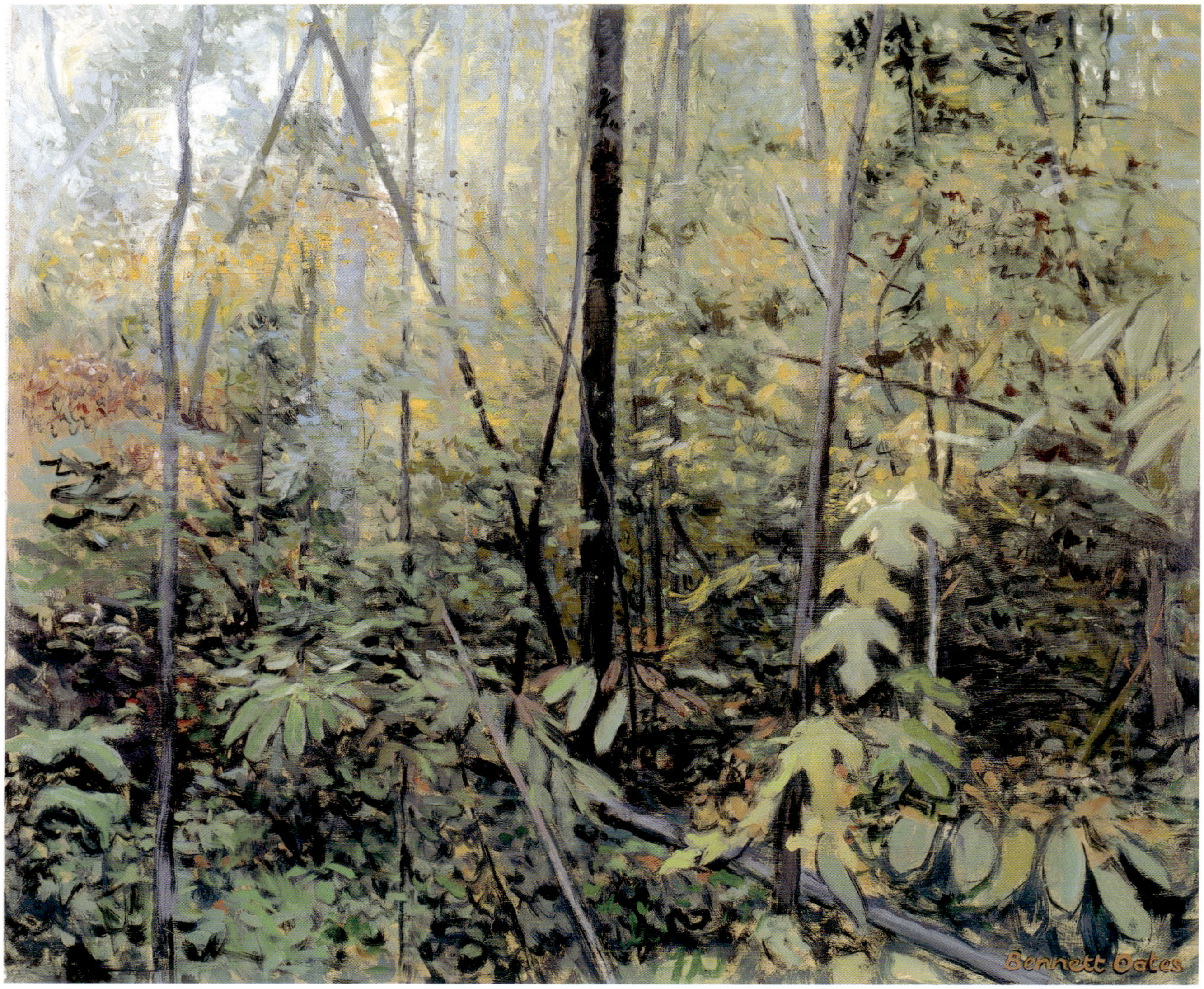

RORY'S WOOD, NORTH CAROLINA

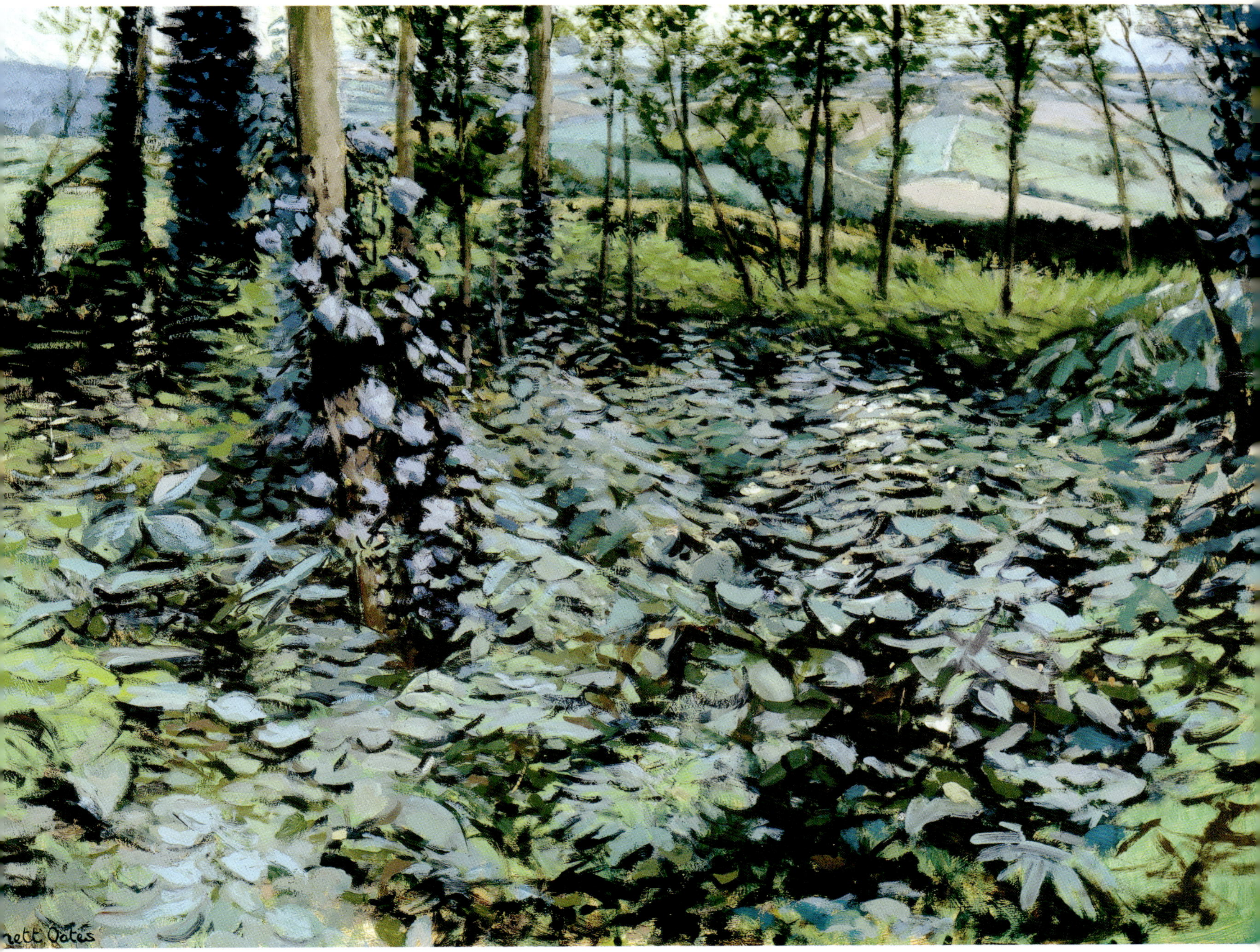

CHIANTI LANDSCAPE

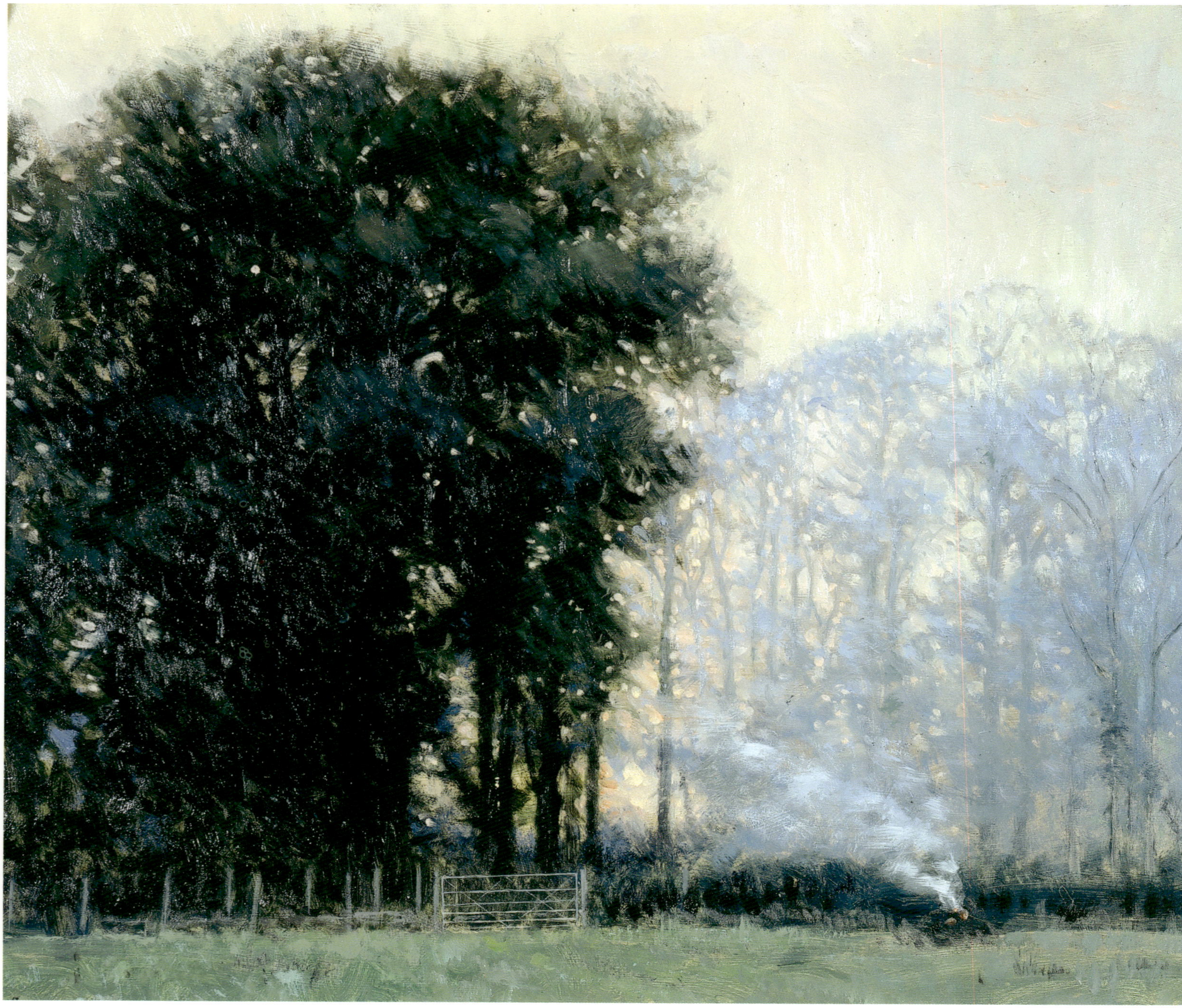

DUSK, LITTLE PLUMSTEAD, NORFOLK

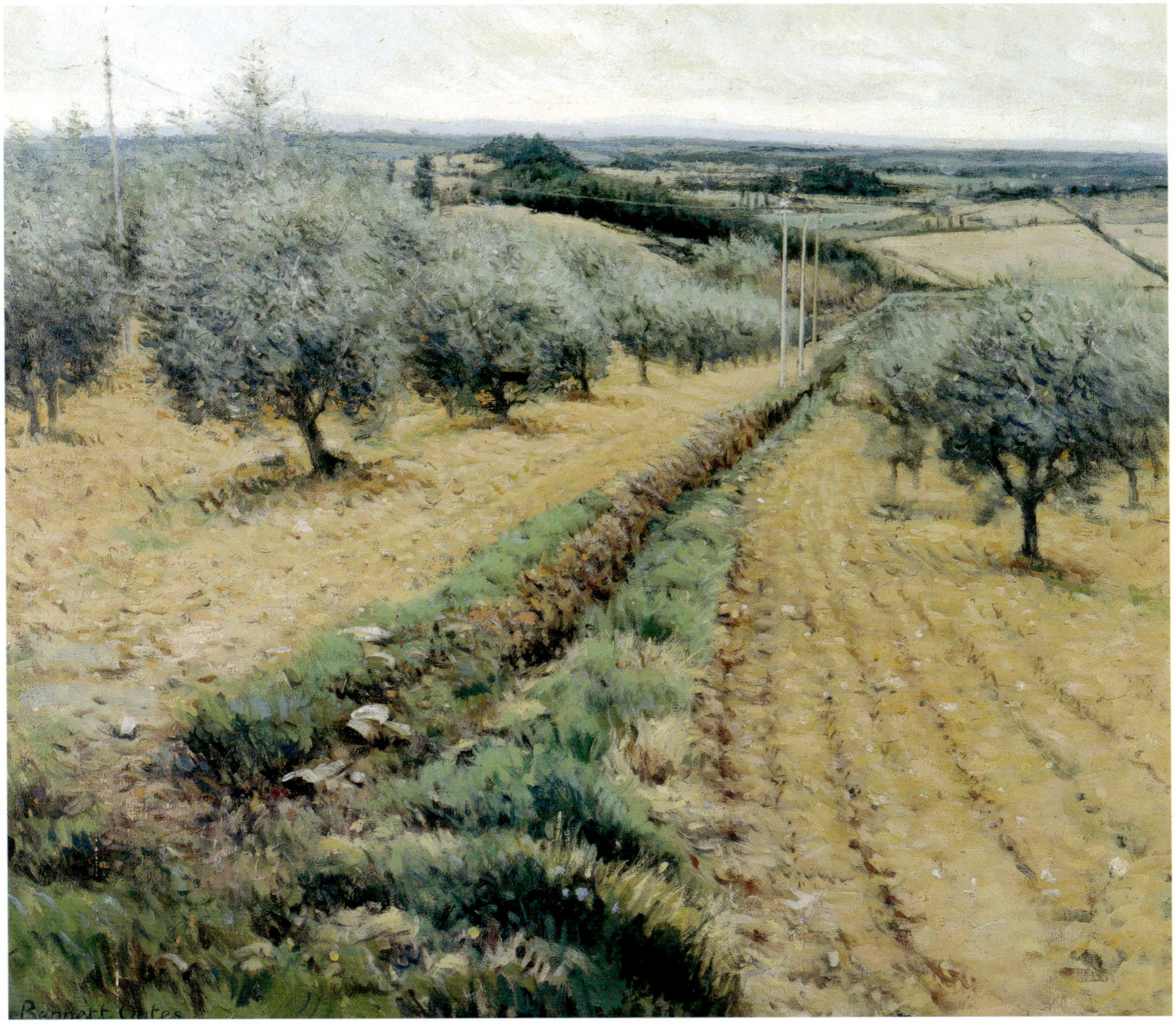

TUSCAN LANDSCAPE

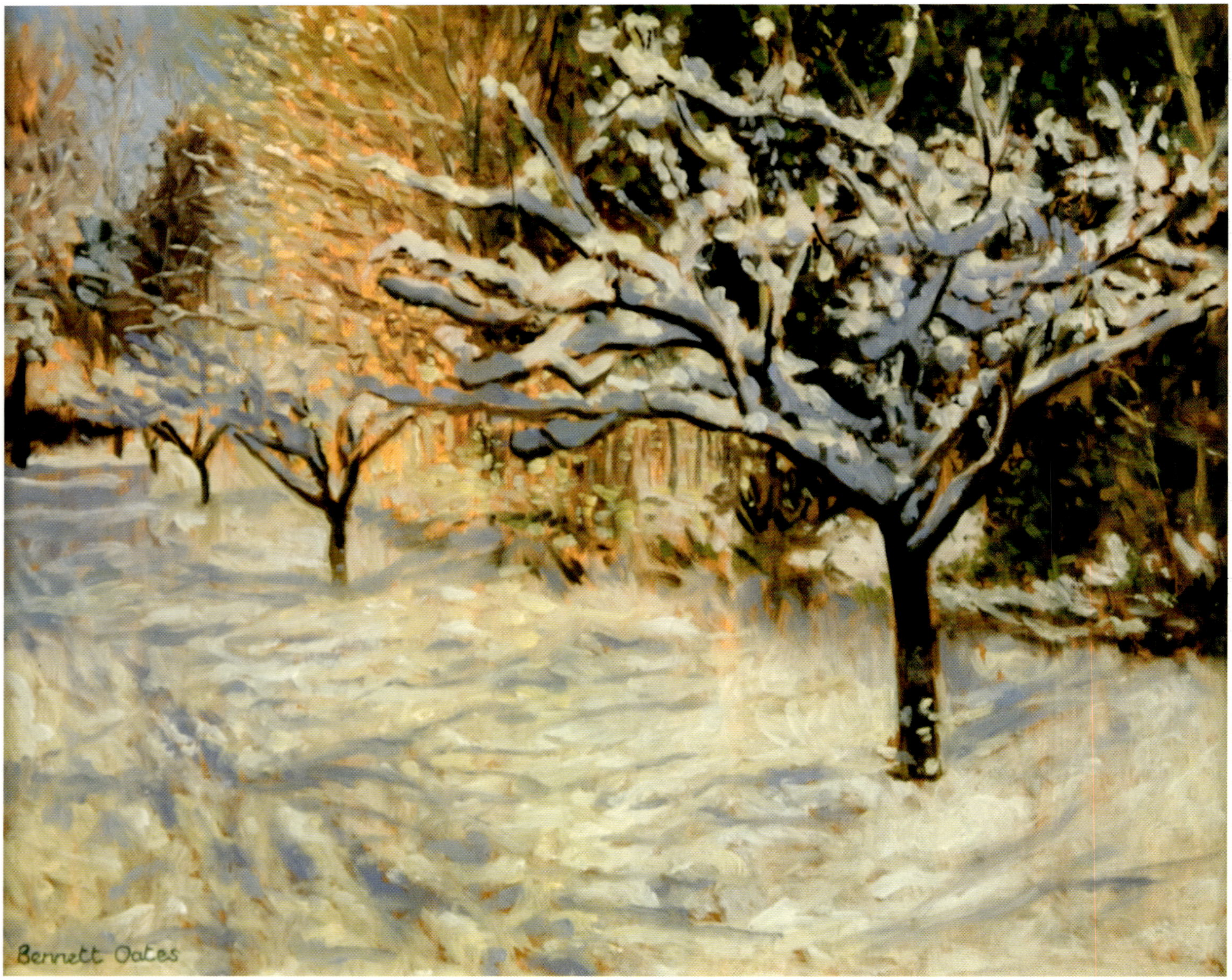

SNOW IN THE ORCHARD

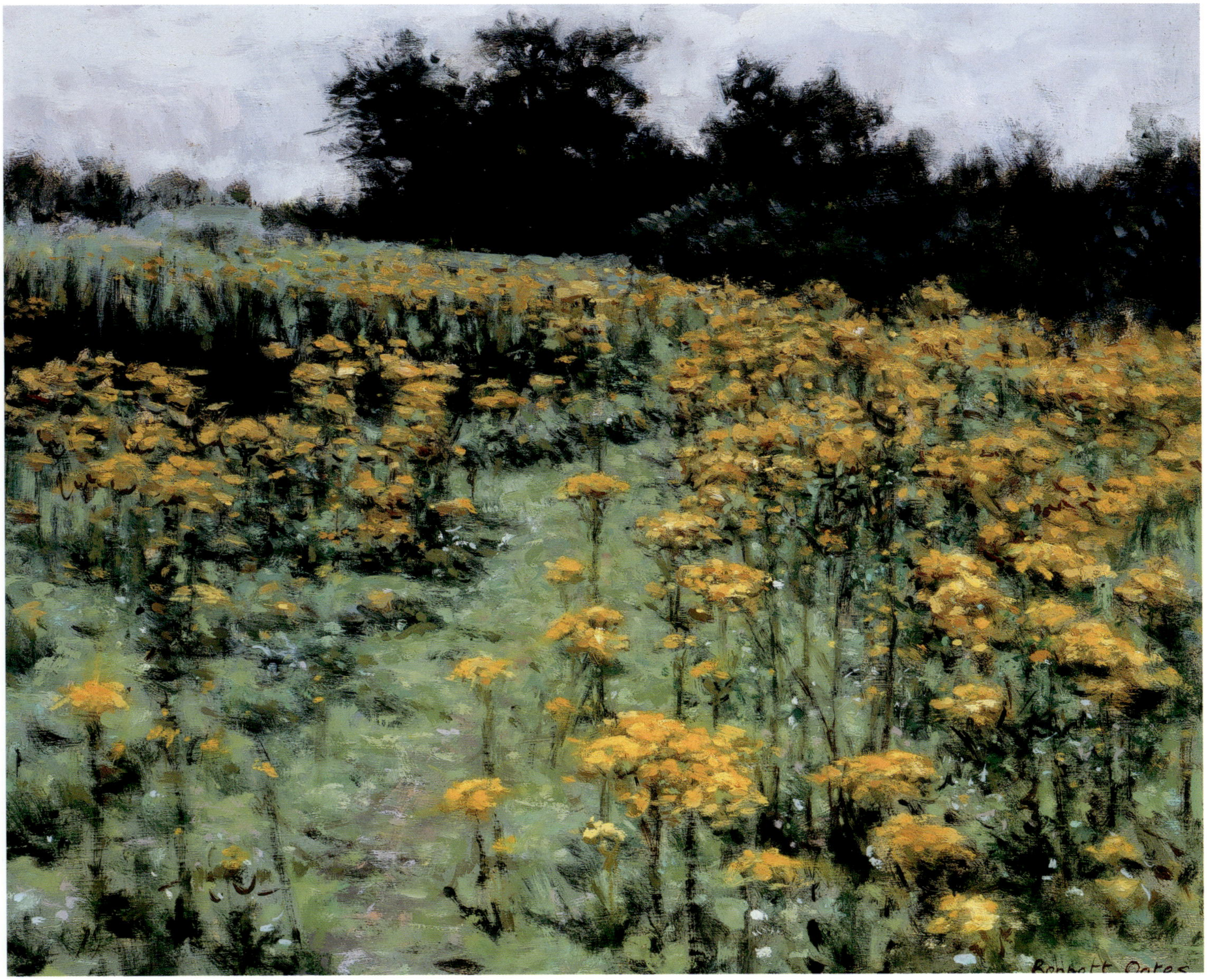

RAGWORT

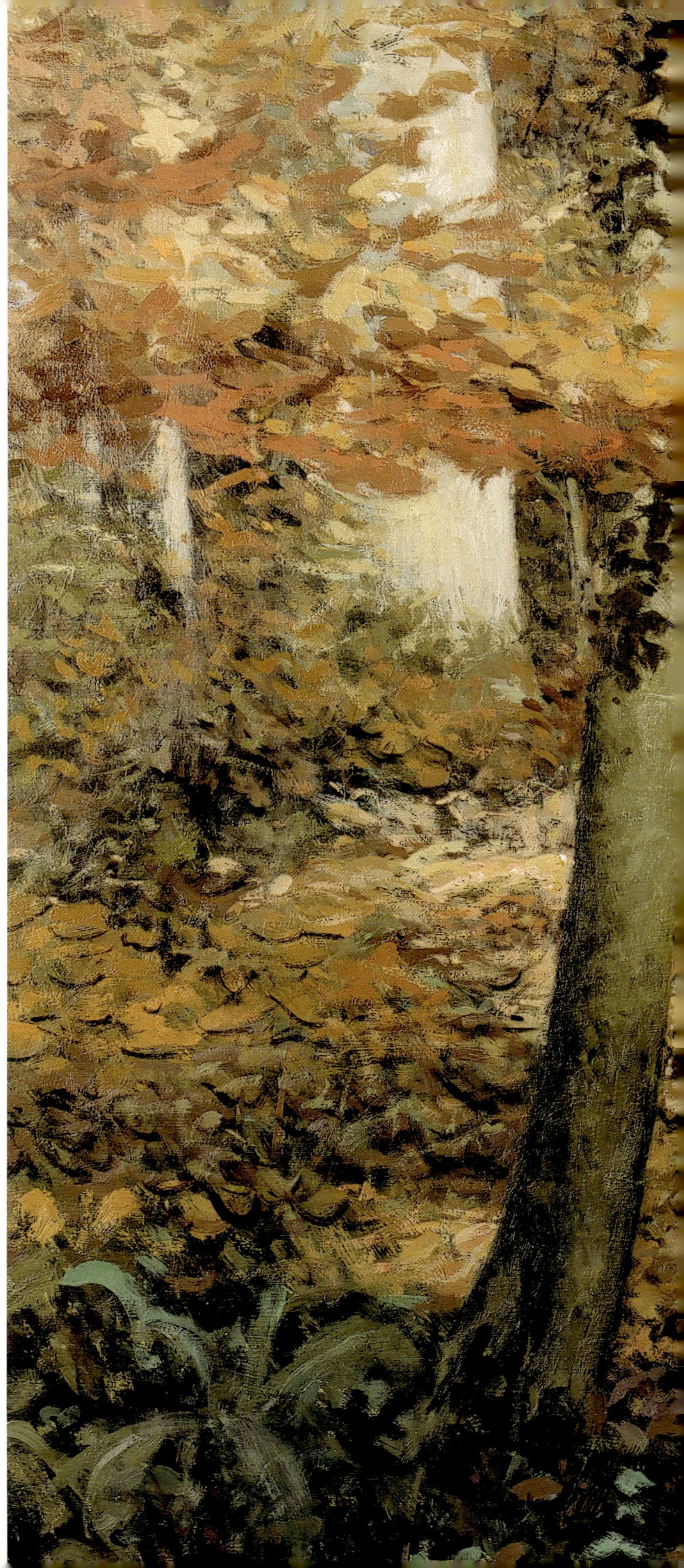

AUTUMN WOODLAND,
PLUMSTEAD, NORFOLK

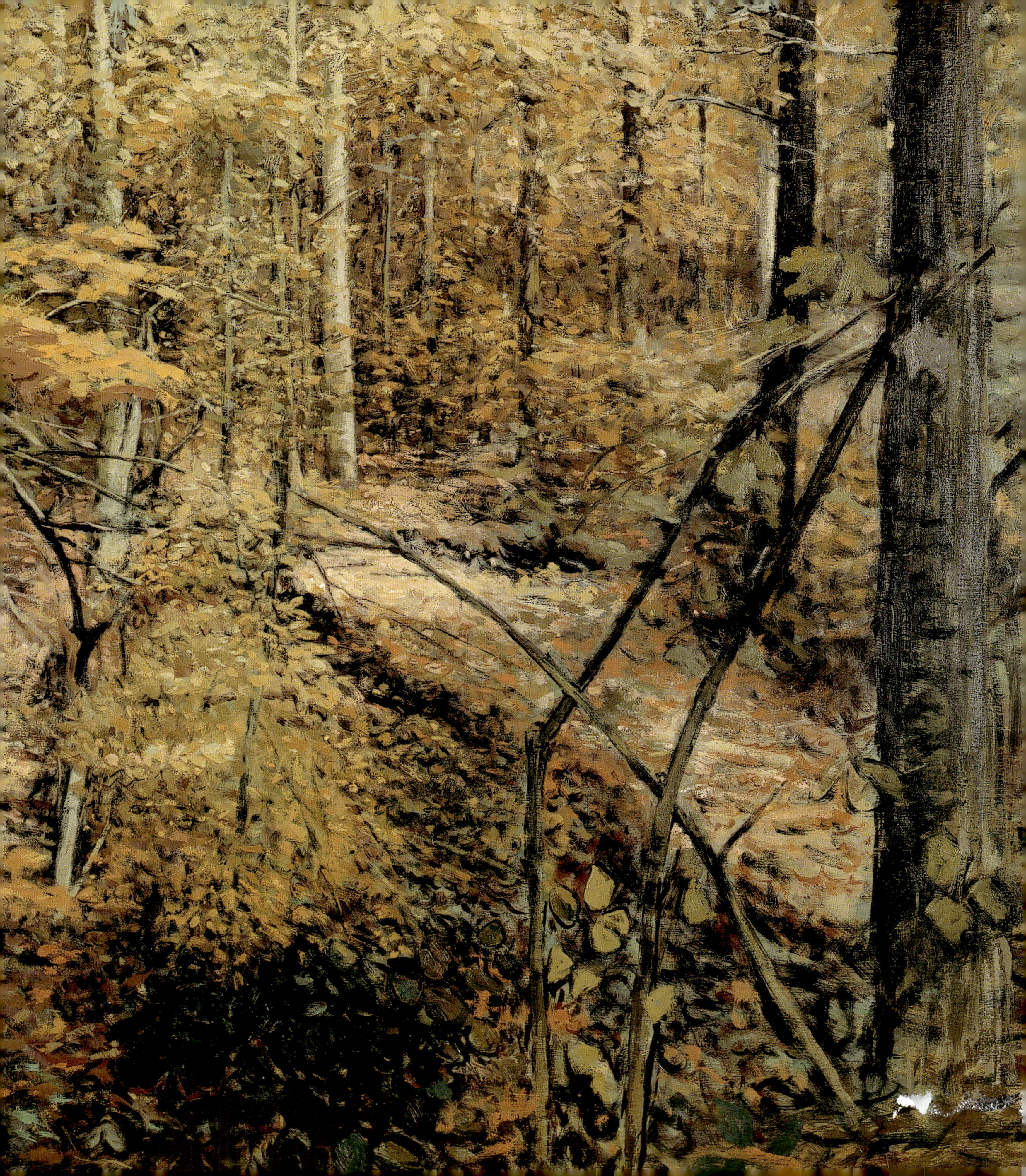

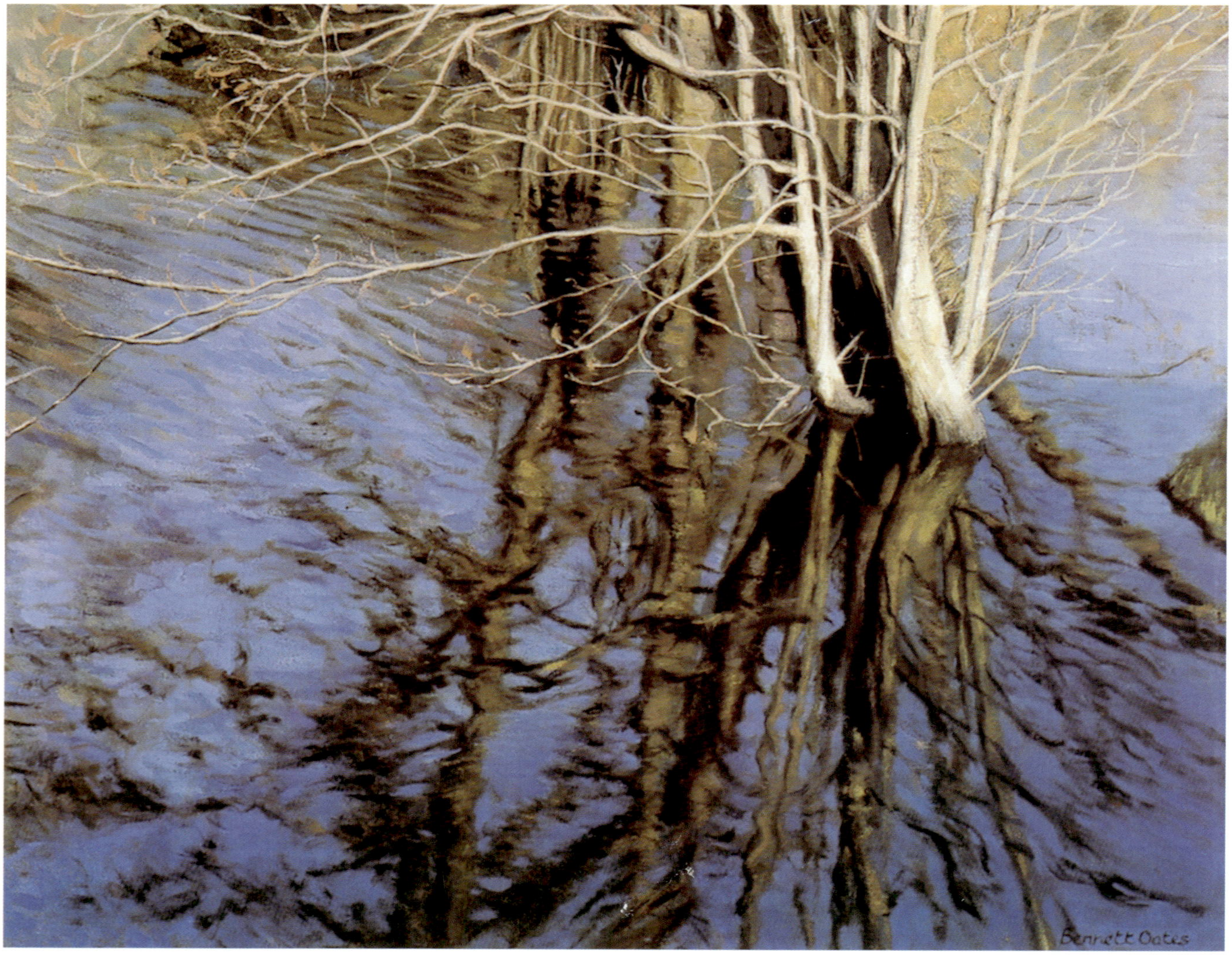

REFLECTIONS 1

MICHELLE BENNETT OATES

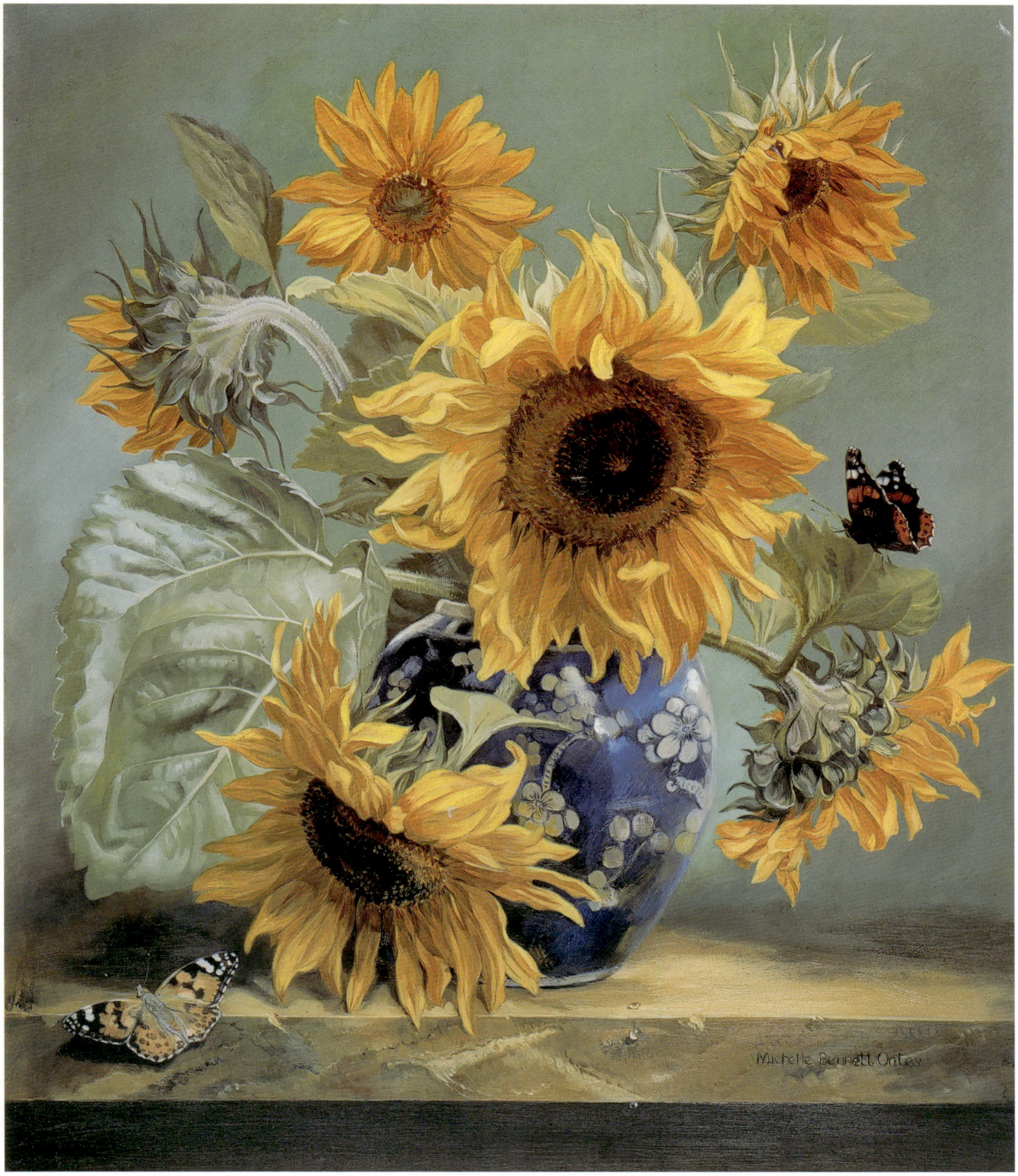

THE FUTURE

DESIGN AND LAYOUT: BEN CRACKNELL STUDIOS, NORWICH
PRINTED: BLACKWELL PRINT, GREAT YARMOUTH, NORFOLK